EXCESS BAGGAGE

ONE WOMAN, ONE MOTORBIKE
AND A HUGE AMOUNT OF LUGGAGE
RIDE ACROSS AUSTRALIA

BY

Jill Maden

For Connie, Kathleen and Harold – thank you

Contents

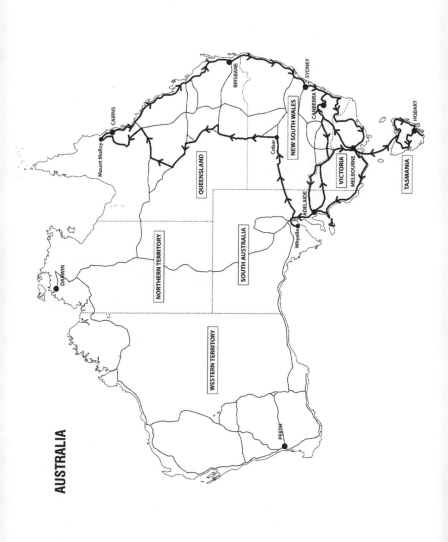

Prologue

REALITY BITES

"Is that you on the big yellow bike?" asked the man on the deck beside me. "Yes," I said, anxiously staring down at the quay, watching the other vehicles being loaded onto the ferry. "Hmm," he said, "I wouldn't fancy carrying all that gear – looks very unstable. I've been watching all the bikes and I thought, no, I definitely wouldn't want to be on that one." My nerves were already in shreds, so this came as no comfort whatsoever. In less than an hour I would have to go back down to the car deck, get onto the "big yellow bike" and ride to Adelaide – something I was dreading. Riding into the heart of a major city when I could barely manage an empty country road seemed like madness, but it was the only answer. I had to do something about my luggage and a big city was my best option for finding a shop that could offer a solution.

I had two very big bags strapped to the seat behind me and a top box on a rack behind them. I was used to riding a Triumph Bonneville T100, a classic touring bike with a low centre of gravity and a single seat for driver and load (whether it be a passenger or luggage). The Suzuki I was now riding had more of a sports bike design, with a higher centre of gravity and a split seat. This meant my luggage was a good couple of inches higher than I was and, with one bag piled on top of the other, it was forming a tall, heavy tower, making the bike very unstable and difficult to handle. Consequently, within two weeks I'd gone from being a fairly experienced and confident rider to a snivelling, nervous wreck.

This wasn't quite what I'd had in mind when planning the trip. In my head, I'd been soaring along wide, open highways, with the sun in my hair and the wind at my back, gently cruising through the twists and turns of Australia's magnificent scenery. Struggling to keep the bike upright was definitely not what I'd imagined when I announced to my friend Minna-Ella, four years previously, that I was going to ride around Australia in 2010.

And now here I was, standing on the top deck of the Kangaroo Island ferry, crapping myself. No, things were definitely not working out as I had planned.

Chapter 1: Aussie Addict

LIVING IN A LAND DOWNUNDER

It had to be Australia. I could have said, "I'm going to ride across Canada," or "Route 66" or "down the Pan-American Highway", all trips I'd considered at some stage or another, but no, it had to be Oz. I'd been out to Australia a few times and completely fallen for it. The weather, the people and the diversity of its landscape all had me hooked and, like a junkie, I always yearned for more. Until Minna-Ella asked, I just hadn't realised I was ready for another fix.

My first visit there was in 1989, when my friend Sue and I went for a year's working holiday.

Early on in the trip we took an eighteen-day four-wheel drive tour from Perth, through the outback, to Darwin. We travelled through incredibly remote parts of the country, accessible only by dirt track, and saw some of the most spectacular sights.

When we arrived in Darwin, Sue decided to join another tour to Alice Springs and Ayres Rock, but I was exhausted and wanted to rest up for a few days. One of the other people on the trip, an Australian girl called Lisa with whom I'd got friendly, also stayed on in Darwin. It turned out we both fancied working on a prawn trawler, something it was possible to do from Darwin. The next day, we went down to the docks and started asking the boats if they had any work. The second boat we asked offered us jobs, but it was leaving that afternoon. As there weren't many other boats to ask, we quickly abandoned our plans of rest and relaxation and accepted their offer.

We spent almost a month at sea and, by the end of the trip, Lisa and I were firm friends.

This was the start of what turned out to be a fun-filled, adventure-packed trip. Being in Australia was the best thing I'd ever done and it left me with a longing for more.

FURTHER WEST THAN STRANRAER

By 2001, things weren't going quite so well. I was 38, back in Glasgow, and had just broken up with my boyfriend of three years. I'd never wanted kids, but the tiny part of me that thought it might be nice knew that my last chance had just disappeared and I was sad about that. Another part of me was sad because it knew it might be a long time before I met somebody else (my track record wasn't that good).

At that time, I was working in information technology and hating it, so when my friend Steve sent me an email saying he'd like to make it "further west than Stranraer" that year, I suggested going to America.

Steve was one of my favourite people. He was ten years younger than me but we'd always got on really well and I loved his company.

After a few years abroad, he'd settled in London, so I didn't get to see him very often, therefore this seemed like a good opportunity to spend some time with him.

He was up for this trip so we booked our tickets for the end of September 2001 to take in New York, Washington, Baltimore and Chicago (all places I had lived in or visited when I was younger). On 11 September 2001, the biggest terrorist attack ever to occur on mainland US soil took place and the Twin Towers of the World Trade Centre in New York were destroyed.

We didn't know what to do. Should we stay or should we go? After some discussion, we decided to go. Our first stop was New York, and while we were there we went down to Ground Zero and saw the remains of the Towers. As I gazed on in disbelief I had a "life is too short" moment and decided that when I got back I would quit my job and do something I'd enjoy that would make a difference in the world.

So I became a massage therapist. I spent the next six years struggling to make a living that way. I tried working in a number of different clinics, but it was really difficult to make enough money to live on. I started to think that if I could control a lot of the aspects of clinic life I currently had no part in, I'd be more successful, and decided that what I really wanted was to have my own clinic.

BIKES

In 2002, Lisa and her husband Lou came to visit me in Scotland and I promised I would go back and visit them again in 2004. I'd been back to Australia in 1992 for my friend Rod's wedding, but hadn't managed to spend much time there. So this time, I went back for five weeks.

The day I arrived in Melbourne, Lisa had to work, so Lou offered to take me down the Great Ocean Road on the back of his Triumph Sprint motorcycle (seeing as we were both British). When I was seventeen, I'd had a biker boyfriend who used to scare the living daylights out of me, hurtling round bends trying to scrape the centre stand off the road surface. We had several crashes, so my latest memories of being on a bike weren't very positive.

However, Lou was a fantastic rider – really steady and stable – and I felt totally safe in his care. In fact, I had such a great day that when I got back to Scotland I decided to look into what was involved in learning how to ride a motorcycle.

I took a trial lesson, which I managed to survive, apart from dropping the bike as soon as I put my leg over the seat. I'd been doing a lot of cycling and was used to lowering the bike down to one side to swing my leg over it. I had done the same thing with the motorbike, not realising it was considerably heavier, and before I could stop it, it got away from me and crashed to the ground with me underneath it.

Undeterred, I signed up for the restricted licence course (which lets you ride a 125 cc bike). I managed to pass the test on my first attempt and immediately went out and bought myself a Kymco 125 cc bike. It was November 2004 by now and winter was fast approaching, but, determined to build up my confidence, I went out in all weathers.

By Easter of the following year, I was starting to feel quite confident. Then I bumped into a guy I used to know when I had the teenage biker boyfriend. He had just done up an old Suzuki GSX450 and was looking to sell it. Thinking this would be the perfect next step for me, I offered to buy it. However, it turned out my restricted licence wouldn't cover it, so I had to take more lessons and upgrade to the full licence.

Having sailed through the restricted test, the full licence proved to be a lot more difficult. I just could not master the U-turn. It took me four attempts at the test before I passed (not because I messed up the U-turn, but because I was so worried about messing up the U-turn that I messed up other things). However, by the time I passed I'd completely nailed it and felt I was really mastering control of a bike.

ADVENTURE MOTORCYCLING

Towards the end of 2005, a new girl, Minna-Ella, started at work. She was from Finland and I liked her immediately. She was bright and funny and, as I'd been introduced to her as "being into bikes", we immediately established a common interest. She had a bike licence (they issued them automatically with a car licence when she was a teenager in Finland) but no bike, and had never even ridden one. She was determined to get a Harley-Davidson, though, and started taking some lessons so she'd know how to ride it when she got one.

We began hanging out together. This was around the time that Ewan McGregor and Charley Boorman did their *Long Way Round* trip. We had both been inspired by this, and when Minna-Ella announced that she was going home to Finland for the summer, we started talking about the possibility of riding over there together.

Shortly after, I happened to walk into the Triumph showroom. They had a gorgeous blue and ivory Bonneville T100 there. I took it for a test run and immediately fell in love. Before I knew it, I'd traded in the Suzuki and was the proud owner of a one-year-old ex-demonstration Bonny. About a week later, Minna-Ella got her Harley-Davidson, so the trip to Finland suddenly became a real possibility and we started planning in earnest.

In June 2006 we set off for Newcastle and got the ferry to Kristiansand in Norway. We rode up through Norway, turned right and headed east for Stockholm in Sweden, where we caught the ferry to Turku in Finland. From there, we continued to Helsinki.

The original plan was to spend two months in Scandinavia and ride up to the North Cape together, but unfortunately I had to leave after a month as there had been some complications with the sale of my flat. When Minna-Ella returned at the end of the summer, she asked me, "So what's your next trip going to be?"

I was as surprised as she was when I found myself saying, "I'm going to ride round Australia in 2010."

Yes, 2010 – that would give me four years to save up enough money to do it.

BARKING UP THE WRONG TREE

But first, I wanted to set up my own massage clinic. I'd made a good profit on the sale of my flat, so now I had the money to finance this venture.

By mid-2007, I'd found the perfect building. I spent a month transforming it from a run-down shell into a beautiful, modern therapy centre. The result was far better than anything I'd imagined and I was absolutely thrilled with it.

I spent the next year putting my heart and soul into building my business. Unfortunately, by the end of its first year the clinic still wasn't breaking even – in fact it was losing money – so, as I had an opportunity to get out of the lease, I made the decision to close it down. I was devastated.

I continued doing massage for the next two years, but my heart just wasn't in it anymore. I realised I'd got totally sucked into the idea that success would make me happy, and when I didn't achieve it and crashed and burned so spectacularly, I was forced to re-assess what really fulfils people.

I realised I'd been barking up the wrong tree – love is what makes people happy. And I don't just mean romantic love, but love in all its forms – fun, laughter, joy, friendship, excitement. And I definitely needed more of that in my life. But I couldn't find it at home; there were too many reminders of what had happened. I needed to do something completely different, in a land where nobody knew me or my history and where I could find myself again. And Australia was calling me back – I just had no idea how I was going to finance it.

PENNIES FROM HEAVEN

During the last months of my clinic, my grandmother died. She was almost 103 and we were all beginning to think she'd live forever. Unfortunately, a leg infection finally got the better of her and rather suddenly brought an end to her time with us.

It turned out that she had left me some money in her will. It took until June 2010 for that money to come through, but when it did, I knew exactly what I was going to do with it. I was 47, single, three stone overweight, battered and bruised, and had totally lost my way in life. I needed something to get me out of my rut. Australia was on!

Chapter 2: The Plan

HOUSE-SITTING

Although I'd been thinking about the trip for four years, by the time I made up my mind to do it, I only had three months to get organised. I needed to put some distance between myself and everything that had happened. Also, I wanted to take my time and really explore the continent, so I knew I wanted to go for a year.

As this was quite a long period of time, I thought house-sitting would be a great way to keep my costs down and see parts of the country I'd never visited before. Plus, most house-sits involved looking after people's pets and, as I loved animals, this seemed like a delightful way to spend my time. Obviously, I'd need a motorbike to get from one house-sit to another, but other than that I hadn't really thought too much about the details of being in Australia for so long.

As soon as my visa came through, I joined a house-sitting website and fixed up a three-month sit on a farm just a few hours' drive from Melbourne. I couldn't believe my luck. I would be near Lisa and Lou in Melbourne (both from farming stock, if anything should go wrong) and I was going to be looking after a farm full of rescued animals – what joy.

TRANSPORTATION

I considered various options regarding a motorbike. I could either take my Triumph, or buy or rent another bike when I arrived. I loved my Triumph: it had a low centre of gravity and so was easy to handle, it looked beautiful and had already accompanied me on two trips abroad, although the last one hadn't been a great success. Earlier in the year, I'd gone with Minna-Ella to Europe, when she was taking her bike back to Finland again. Before we even got on the ferry at Newcastle, mine started losing power. Determined not to miss out on another adventure, I forced it through Holland, but by the time we got to Germany it was only firing on one cylinder and I could barely keep it at 60 mph on the motorways, so I had to abandon Minna-Ella and turn back.

The bike and I limped back to the ferry at Amsterdam. As we came off at the other end, the bike seemed to lose power altogether and I could hardly get it to move. Instead of doing the sensible thing and calling breakdown assistance, I cranked on the accelerator and burned up the clutch getting it to pull off. We crawled our way at 10 mph through Newcastle, back onto the road north.

All of a sudden I thought I could smell something burning. I looked down and discovered the exhaust was on fire. I pulled into the first lay-by I could find, called the AA and ended up getting towed all the way back to Glasgow. Although the fault was later fixed, my faith in the bike's mechanical integrity had been slightly dented.

But taking the Bonny was what I really wanted to do, so I looked into shipping it over to Australia. Although the costs wouldn't have been prohibitive, there were some logistical issues that were going to make it very difficult.

In order to temporarily take a motor vehicle out of the European Union, you need to have a *Carnet de Passage en Douanes*, and to get a Carnet, the vehicle must remain registered in the country of origin for the entire time it is out of the country. To keep it registered in the UK, it has to be taxed, insured and have a valid MOT. My road tax and MOT would run out while I was away, which would mean I wouldn't be able to renew them in Australia. This would therefore breach the terms of the Carnet, meaning I wouldn't be able to re-import the bike back to the UK at the end of the trip.

Next I looked into renting a bike. This seemed like quite a good idea, as the rental company would be responsible, should any breakdowns occur. The down side was that the money paid on rental would not be recoverable at the end of the trip and the rider was also responsible for all servicing and replacement parts. However, I didn't write off this idea altogether.

Lastly, I could buy something when I got there. This had the advantages that I could sell it again at the end of my trip and recoup some of my expenses, and that it was fully my responsibility. So I decided to buy a bike when I got there (or rent if I couldn't find one).

Then there was the small matter of getting my flat ready to be rented out while I was away. This turned out to be an incredibly time-consuming affair. By the time I'd packed and moved all my personal possessions into storage and made sure everything met every standard and condition imaginable, I only had about a week to think about what I'd need to take.

Sometime during the final month before I was due to depart, I got an email from the owner of the farm I'd be sitting, saying she was terribly sorry, but her trip to India had been cancelled and she would no longer require me to look after her farm. *Oh my God – what a disaster.*

I knew I couldn't just turn up at my friends' in Melbourne and stay indefinitely. I had to have somewhere to go when I arrived. So I got back on the web and started madly applying for every house-sit I could find. Two people offered me sits and, bless them, Lisa and Lou came to the rescue by asking if I would look after their two dogs for a month so that they could take a holiday too.

So all was well. I would arrive in Australia on 11 September 2010 and spend two weeks with my friends in Melbourne. They would then go on holiday for four weeks and I'd stay on to look after their dogs (giving me a total of six weeks in Melbourne to find a motorcycle). After that, I'd head up to Lake Boga in northern Victoria for my next house-sit, then on to Whyalla in South Australia for another week's house-sit over Christmas. Perfect! I was all set.

Chapter 3: Overloaded

LOSING THE PLOT

I've always prided myself on being a light traveller, but somehow I lost the plot with this trip. The fact that I was going to be away for a year seemed to give me permission to take anything I wanted.

I decided I would take my existing motorcycle gear, as it was in good condition and buying new kit in Australia would cost a fortune. For weeks, I vacillated between taking my gorgeous, well-cut Triumph leather jacket, which had the insulating properties of a hairnet but looked as cool as anything, and my all-weather Shelltex fabric jacket, which had numerous pockets and removable liners that could be added or taken away depending on the temperature but was enormous and made me look like a big black Michelin Man.

Motorcycling isn't just about whizzing along wide, open roads; it's about looking good as you whiz along them. Every motorcyclist seems to develop their own unique style – for instance, Minna-Ella had a sparkly purple, open-faced helmet which she wore with a flying jacket, suede trousers and cowboy boots, making her look like something out of *Easy Rider*. I, on the other hand, had adopted something more of a traffic cop look. Whether it was my leather or the Shelltex, I was all in black with a white helmet and sometimes a hi-visibility bib. What I couldn't decide was, should I sacrifice style for practicality? Eventually, I opted for practicality and squeezed my Shelltex jacket and all its liners into my kit bag. Along with it went my helmet, boots, trousers, gloves, neck-warmer and a set of billy cans for camping.

I wasn't sure whether I should take a full set of camping gear too. Obviously, next to house-sitting, camping would be the cheapest way to travel, but it was very bulky and I wasn't sure I wanted to be laden down with so much equipment. But a tent and sleeping bag would always provide a useful fall-back, should alternative forms of accommodation not be available. Eventually I compromised with myself – I would leave the tent and post the sleeping bag.

Clothes were the next dilemma. I would be arriving in the spring and staying for all three remaining seasons, so I'd need warm clothes as well as cool ones. My biggest mistake was to take two colour ranges. I had one set of clothes that was mostly blues, greens and purples, and another that was mainly browns, beiges and creams. The browns, beiges and creams turned out to be an unnecessary extravagance and created the next problem – shoes.

What colour shoes should I take? I'd need something that would match all these colours and be wearable in both hot and cold weather. That meant at least one pair of sandals and a pair of trainers, but the colour matching was proving difficult so I ended up having to add an extra pair of sandals. Plus, I'd need something to match that new green dress I'd bought, so in went a pair of green sandals as well. And, of course, I'd need some nice dresses to wear when I wasn't riding, and sun tops and shorts. Not to mention underwear and appropriate bras to wear under the sun tops and dresses. Oh, and a bikini and, of course, a sarong to cover my flabby bits. And a towel – God, I almost forgot a towel!

And what if it was cold? I'd need some cardigans for that. And everything had to match and coordinate with everything else. And what about toiletries and perhaps a few items of jewellery for when I wanted to look nice? Oh, and there was that hair curler I'd recently got, which made me look all girly and pretty. Because, let's face it, a girl likes to look good after a hard day's motorcycling. And so it was that I managed to fill a second enormous bag.

And it didn't end there. Oh no, there was still my laptop, camera, cables, adaptors, tool kit, bungees, first aid kit, guide books, map and study materials for the two Open University courses I'd decided to study whilst doing the farm-sit (although that was now cancelled, I was still committed to doing the courses). These filled another small backpack. Not to mention a selection of "small" gifts I'd been given, which people thought I'd be able to stash easily in small nooks and crannies in my bags.

I could barely lift each individual case, let alone carry the whole lot. On weighing them, I discovered they amounted to a total of seven stone: the weight of a small adult. I'd only ever taken a pillion passenger on three occasions and found it very difficult to control the bike, so this did not bode well for a lap around one of the largest countries in the world.

LEAVING

I left Glasgow on Tuesday 31 August 2010. My parents had divorced before I went to Australia the first time and were both now remarried and living in different parts of the country. I decided to take the train down to London instead of flying, which would allow me to stop and say my farewells to them and some friends along the way.

My friend Alicia picked me up from my flat and took me to the train station. We lugged all my bags into her car and set off. Glasgow Central is a beautiful old Victorian railway station with a special vehicle entrance passing through a tunnel up to an area by the platforms where people can be dropped off. Out of all the times I've been there, I've always been able to get in via this entrance, but on this occasion, when I had a mountain of heavy luggage, it was shut. We ended up having to park several streets away.

Christ, I thought as we heaved it all out of Alicia's car. How the hell are we going to get all this into the station? Alicia took the backpack and, as one bag had wheels on it, I was able to put the other one on top of it and drag them behind me. But it was hardly a stable assembly, and hauling them across Glasgow's crowded streets left a trail of bruised and battered pedestrians in our wake.

"Oops, sorry," I exclaimed repeatedly, as I pulled my load up the stairs into the main concourse, breaking into a sweat before we were able to secure a baggage trolley.

Gasping for breath, we wheeled our way over to the café, where another friend, Lesley, joined us for lunch and to wave me off. Alicia, Lesley and I (together with a group of other women) had all worked together twenty years previously and we'd kept in touch ever since. They were two of my oldest friends and it was sad leaving them behind, especially as I wasn't sure if I'd ever come back again. But I was too excited to dwell on it for long.

First stop was the Lake District to see my dad. Thankfully all the luggage racks in my compartment were full, which meant I didn't have to carry my bags beyond the doorway of the train, where I piled them up in a neat stack.

Getting everything off the train at Oxenholme and dragging it all through the subterranean tunnel to the platform from which my connecting train was due to depart in four minutes was a panic-stricken affair. First I had to find a luggage trolley, then heap everything onto it and try to stop the trolley running away from me as we hurtled down the tunnel, only to have to push it back up the hill at the other side. A friendly conductor helped me throw the last bag onto the train just as the doors were closing.

Phew, I made it. But the drama didn't end there. When I arrived in Windermere, my step-mother's car couldn't accommodate the three of us plus all the luggage, and I had to walk to their house while they transported my gear. At this point, I really began to worry that I'd overdone it with the packing.

I managed to shed a few items whilst staying at my dad's. The green sandals went, as did some of the brown, beige and cream clothes, the hair curlers and some massage oil I'd brought just in case. But it didn't make a lot of difference and by the time I left I still had three very large, heavy bags.

During my time there, I discovered that my dad had just had a pacemaker fitted. He hadn't bothered telling me about this beforehand and it was only when I hugged him that he explained he couldn't use his left arm properly as he might pull the stitches out. Apparently he'd been suffering from an irregular heartbeat for a long time and his doctor had suggested that a pacemaker might help. Dad seemed to be making a good recovery, but it left me feeling a bit concerned about his overall health.

In London, I checked the bag with the bike gear into Left Luggage at Euston Station and met up with Steve. As we made our way across London to his flat, I could feel my neck straining to counterbalance the weight of the books in my backpack. The next day, when I went to meet another friend, Sheila, and almost tore the muscle in my neck, I really started panicking.

My final stop in the UK before Heathrow Airport was Hemel Hempstead, to see my mum. This station didn't even have a ramp – just a long set of stairs. It took two trips to get my bags from the platform to my mum's car.

I'd had a strange, nagging doubt that I was only going to be allowed to check one piece of luggage into the aircraft's hold. I'd already asked the travel agents and they'd assured me it would be fine to take two pieces, but something was telling me that this might not be true. When I got to my mum's, I went online to check this out and, sure enough, I was only allowed one piece. Fortunately, I could take the excess bag if I paid an extra fee and checked in online, which I duly did.

My route from the UK to Australia went west, via San Francisco, where I had a couple of days' stopover. Again, I checked the bike-gear bag into Left Luggage at the airport and dragged the other pair of bags into the centre of town to my accommodation.

ARRIVING

Touching down in Melbourne, even the sniffer dogs were suspicious of my cargo. I was pulled aside and questioned, but it seemed they were more interested in whether I was carrying any foodstuffs than how many bags I had. As food was the one thing I hadn't brought, I could confidently deny any such wrong-doing. I might have had everything, including the kitchen sink (I was actually carrying a small, collapsible kitchen sink for washing camping dishes), but I definitely was not carrying any food. Sniffer wasn't convinced, however, but thankfully he only honed in on the small backpack, which was relatively easy to unpack and repack again to prove my innocence.

Outside, I waited for Lisa to arrive. It was cold in Melbourne. I'd timed my trip to arrive in the spring, so I was expecting it to be quite warm, but it seemed it was still the end of winter, with a temperature to match. As I stood there shivering, I realised the one thing I hadn't packed was a fleece.

There was a long queue of cars pulling up to collect friends and relatives, so when Lisa arrived she wasn't able to pull in. She honked her horn and waved as she drove by. I thought she was indicating that she was going to do a circuit and come round again, but after about fifteen minutes there was still no sign of her and I realised this wasn't so.

Soon I noticed a pale car, way off in the distance, with a woman standing beside it, waving. It was Lisa. I bolted down the walkway to meet her. Hugs and kisses were exchanged and I was introduced to her baby daughter Eva, who was in a car seat in the back.

Oh God, I hope this isn't going to be a repeat of the Windermere saga, I thought, as Lisa opened the boot. I was immensely relieved to see that it was empty and we were able to squeeze all my stuff inside. I had to laugh, though, when she told me that my sleeping bag had arrived in the post the previous day. How on earth was I ever going to pile all this gear onto a motorcycle?

Chapter 4: Bike Shopping

WARM WELCOMES

I was so pleased to see Lisa again. We'd had so many adventures together and I'd always thought of her as a kindred spirit. She was a year younger than me: tall, slim with short brown hair. One of my favourite things about her was her sense of outrage. When I first met her, I had a tendency to say things like, "The trouble with such-and-such a subject is ...", to which she would balk back, "That's a gross generalisation based on one isolated incident; you don't really know that."

I quickly learnt that I needed to get my facts straight before I started saying such things around Lisa, but sometimes I would do it just for fun, to see how outraged I could get her. She was a vegetarian and into alternative therapies, so, at the time we met, seemed a bit eclectic to me. But it meant we always had lots to talk about and I really enjoyed her company.

After our prawn trawling experience, the trawler docked at a place on the east coast of Queensland called Mourilyan. Lisa and I made our way to Cairns, where we stayed for the next five months. Initially we stayed in a backpacker's hostel, but soon we moved into a house run by the hostel for longer-term travellers. Two guys who'd been at the hostel, Rod and Shane, also moved in, plus four other people we hadn't met before. We all had a blast together and it turned out to be one the happiest periods of my life.

Shortly after arriving in Cairns, Lisa and I discovered the joys of white-water rafting. Separately, we went on trips down the nearby Barron and Tully Rivers, and I did a five-day trip down the not-so-nearby North Johnson River.

We loved it so much we decided we wanted to become white-water river guides, so we hung around Cairns for months, waiting for a course to start. We started swimming daily to get in shape for the course, and enjoyed all the activities that Cairns had to offer. I learnt to scuba dive and got one job selling tickets for the dodgems at the annual fun fair and another one selling photos of people boarding a pleasure cruiser.

The course was in Tully, a small farming town about 150 km south of Cairns, so Lisa and I moved into a house there run by the rafting company. Although the course was great, somewhere along the way I lost my nerve and didn't stay on to become a guide. I left Tully to meet up with Sue, the friend I'd come out to Australia with, and continued our tour of the country. But Lisa and I stayed in touch and she had become one of those rare friends that I could pick up with where I'd left off.

As we drove back from the airport, Lisa asked, "How was your flight?"

"Oh God," I laughed. "It was ridiculous. There was this Asian girl sitting at the end of my row who didn't get up for the entire journey."

"So?" asked Lisa

"Well, I was in the window seat, so this meant I had to clamber over her and the woman next to me every time I wanted to get out and I wanted to get out quite a lot. On my final attempt," I continued, "I didn't want to wake them up so I decided I'd try to swing myself from my seat to the aisle in one smooth, gymnastic movement."

"Oh my God ..." said Lisa knowing what was coming.

"Well, I didn't quite make it and ended up landing in the Asian girl's lap."

"Hah!" burst out Lisa, then immediately turned it around by saying, "Poor girl, she was probably sitting there thinking, Oh no, what's this stupid woman doing now?"

Pulling up at Lisa's house was a huge relief. After all the strain of transporting my gear halfway round the globe, I had finally arrived and it was wonderful to be with such good friends again. Lisa and Lou immediately made me feel at home, providing cups of tea and a room for me to rest my weary bones.

DICING WITH DEATH

The next day, Lou took me on a Moto Guzzi Owners' Club bike ride to Woodend, in the countryside north of Melbourne. This time, Lou was on a Rossa Corsa, a Moto Guzzi sports bike, with me perched on the back. It wasn't as comfortable as I remembered the Triumph being, and at the first stop I found my knees had completely seized up from being propped on pillion pegs that seemed to be about six inches below the seat.

Noticing that I was having difficulty dismounting, one of the other owners arranged for me to go pillion on the back of his and another rider's bikes, as they had more leg room. The first one was a Moto Guzzi California and the owner had us sweeping through bends so smoothly I almost forgot my usual fear of cornering. The second owner had an even more comfortable bike but was a much faster rider – so much so that we overshot a left turn and had to do a U-turn to rejoin the pack. For some reason, he crossed over onto the right side of the road to do this and then turned straight into the path of a car that was now approaching in the left lane.

The car's driver slammed on his brakes and his wheels squealed as he careered towards us. All I could think about was the pain of taking a full broadside hit, smashing my leg to smithereens and being dragged up the road in a mangled mess of car and motorbike.

God, I'm going to end up in a wheelchair on my first day, I thought in alarm. I couldn't see how we could get out of this. Then, just as I braced myself for impact, my rider had the presence of mind to accelerate onto the grass verge at the side of the road and we missed the car by inches. I sat there on the back for a moment, not quite believing what had happened.

I thought the car driver would stop to see if we were all right, or at least come and yell at us for being such idiots, but he just carried on into the distance as we sank into the bog. I got off the bike as another rider came to our assistance, and together we managed to push it free of the mud.

After that, my driver slowed down a bit and at the next stop I was handed back to Lou's capable charge, who, incidentally, had missed the whole thing and couldn't see what all the fuss was about.

Although it was an exciting way to start my adventure, I couldn't help wondering if this was the universe's way of telling me that motorcycling around Australia wasn't, perhaps, the wisest idea.

This sense of foreboding stayed with me over the next few days, as I tried to buy a bike.

GOING SHOPPING

"So what type of bike do you want?" Lou asked me over breakfast the next morning.

"I'm not really sure," I replied. "Something really light, like a 125 or 250 cc, so if I drop it I'll be able to pick it back up again."

He thought about this and suggested, "You'd probably be better off with something bigger. You'd be able to keep up with the other traffic if you had a bit of power behind you – and it will take you ages to cover any distance on a 125."

"It would also make it easier to transport all my luggage," I agreed.

We had a bit of a debate about whether I should go for a road bike or a trail bike. I'd only ever ridden road bikes and wasn't too keen on the idea of a trail bike as they seemed to be quite tall, with a high centre of gravity which I was worried would be difficult to handle. In the end, Lou clinched it by saying, "If you're going to do the majority of your riding on sealed roads, then you'd be best getting a bike designed for doing that, but if you plan to do most of your riding off-road, then you'd be better getting a trail bike."

Although I quite fancied the idea of doing some off-road riding, I knew I'd be doing the majority of my trip on sealed roads, so I decided a road bike would be the best option.

Lou was 50 now and had been riding bikes since he was a kid. His father was a mechanic, so as well as being a very experienced rider, Lou also knew how bikes worked. He was one of those people who not only know how to take a bike apart but can put it back together again.

Lou seemed very considered in everything he did. He struck me as someone who liked to think things through before making a decision, so I really respected his opinion and found I was relying heavily on him for advice on what to get and where to get it. Although I'd been to Melbourne before, I'd never had to buy a motorcycle there and had no idea where to start.

Later that morning, Lisa and Lou took me into Elizabeth Street in the city centre to look at what the bike shops had to offer. I was shocked to discover how much secondhand bikes cost in Australia.

Lou had sent me some internet adverts when I was still in Glasgow. They had seemed very costly, but, in my ignorance, I didn't believe that all used bikes could be this expensive. It looked as if it would be impossible to buy anything under my budget figure of $5,000 (£3,000). When one guy offered me a twenty-two-year-old Honda for $8,000 (about £5,000), I just laughed out loud.

At one point we saw an old BMW GS650. It looked to be in reasonable condition and, as it was designed for adventure touring, seemed as though it might be the ideal solution. But when I swung my leg over and found my feet couldn't quite reach the ground, I realised there was no way I'd be able to ride it, so that had to be rejected too.

As the afternoon wore on, my jet-lag started to kick in and I became increasingly confused and indecisive about what I wanted. I could tell that Lou was starting to despair with me, so, when I saw the Triumph showroom, I suggested we went in to see how much a new Bonny would cost.

It felt great to see my old friends again, but at $18,000 (£11,000), getting another Bonny was completely out of the question. However, it did put the idea of trying to get a secondhand one into my mind.

So the next day, when Lou came in with a bike sales magazine, I found it difficult to consider anything other than another Triumph. But there was nothing within my price range and, in fact, secondhand Bonnies were proving to be almost as expensive as new ones.

Later that morning, I decided to go back into Melbourne by myself and see if I could find something, without the pressure of having other people with me.

But I didn't see anything new, so I opened a bank account and got a mobile phone instead. As I didn't know many people in Australia and therefore wouldn't have many folk to call, I went for a pre-paid deal. By the end of the day I had a fully functioning new phone, with what was claimed to be the best coverage in Australia.

As I got the train home, I was starting to worry that my adventure would be over before it had begun, because I couldn't find anything affordable. Perhaps the universe really was telling me that the sensible thing to do would be to buy a car instead?

But then, when I got home, Lou said he'd found a Moto Guzzi California for sale on eBay. The pictures looked good and it came with panniers, a top box and a safe (whatever that was). This meant I wouldn't have to buy any luggage containers.

We arranged to go and see it the next day. Unfortunately, it turned out to be in fairly poor condition and also had the twin problems that (a) it had a heel-operated gear lever, which I had never used before and knew I'd find confusing and (b) my legs weren't long enough to reach the foot stand.

It was surprisingly stable, though. The safe turned out to be a lockable steel container between the rear mudguard and the top box. Nevertheless, I decided against it.

On the way back, Lou remembered that there was a Suzuki dealer nearby, so we went to see what they had. Immediately, Lou picked out a bright yellow Suzuki SV650 with upright handlebars. One of the girls on the Moto Guzzi run had had one of these and had let me try it, but because it had dropped handlebars, I didn't find it very comfortable and had rejected it as a choice. However, the upright handlebars made all the difference. I took it for a test ride and, apart from the gear lever being in a different position from the one on my Bonny, which meant I kept missing it, it was nice and light, felt good and was within budget at $4,700 – so I decided to buy it.

You need to have a local address to register a vehicle in Victoria. I gave the lady at the bike shop my driving licence and new bank statement as proof of this and was advised, all being well, that I should be able to pick up the bike on the Friday (two days' time). I couldn't wait.

BEST LAID PLANS

Five days into my trip and already things weren't going quite to plan. Lisa and Lou asked if I could change the time that I'd be house-sitting for them until after I got back from Lake Boga. This meant I'd have two weeks in Melbourne and then four weeks in which to find something else to do. After that, I'd have a week in Lake Boga, followed by another few weeks to occupy myself, and then the house-sit in Whyalla over Christmas. This wouldn't be ideal as it meant I wouldn't have enough time in one place to do my studies, but as Lisa and Lou had been so incredibly helpful in finding the bike and putting me up, I agreed.

There was also bad news from the bike shop. The vehicle registration authority in Victoria, VicRoads, wouldn't accept my driving licence as proof of my address in Australia – which wasn't surprising, really, seeing as it had my UK address on it.

This meant I would need another form of address confirmation. I could use a mobile phone bill, but as I'd just taken out a pre-paid package, I didn't have a bill and would need to change to a monthly contract to get one. After I'd spent an hour or so at the phone shop filling out all the various forms, it transpired that, because I'd now been in Australia for five days, the time remaining on my visa was only 360 days instead of 365, which meant I wasn't eligible for the pay-monthly one-year contract that I'd just taken out.

Being ultra-efficient, the assistant processed the order before discovering this, so the contract then had to be cancelled and a new one set up. However, due to a slight technical hitch he wasn't able to do this straightaway, which meant I'd have to wait till the Monday before he could swap me onto an ad hoc monthly contract instead and get the necessary documentation.

All this would put the collection date for my bike back to the following Wednesday. As Lisa and Lou's young daughter didn't sleep very well (which meant they didn't sleep well either and were somewhat sleep-deprived), I sensed that this news didn't go down too well and worried that I might be getting to the limit of my welcome. Consequently, I felt a sudden need to get on the road as soon as possible, though I hadn't a clue where I should go.

Lou suggested Tasmania, but as it was still freezing on mainland Australia, I wasn't particularly keen on the idea of going even further south and freezing my bits off again. In April, when Minna-Ella and I had gone back to Europe, it was absolutely freezing and proved to be a very bitter ride, so I definitely didn't want a repeat of that experience.

When planning this trip, I'd come across something called the Oodnadatta Track, which is a dirt road that runs from Cooper Pedy in South Australia to the Pink Roadhouse at Oodnadatta and then back to the main road to Darwin at Marla. For some reason, the prospect of seeing a pink roadhouse really appealed to me. However, several people on the internet forum I'd joined advised me against it at this time of year, especially if I was going alone, as it could be prone to flooding.

After great debate, I finally decided to go along the Great Ocean Road. After all, this was where my interest in motorcycling had started six years earlier, when Lou had taken me down it on his Triumph, so it seemed like a fitting place to begin.

BUSH, MOBS, BUCKS AND ANIMAL WELFARE

While waiting for the phone bill to be generated by the phone company, Lisa and I managed to have a day out together. It was great fun and reassured me that I hadn't completely overstayed my welcome.

We went to a place called The Homestead, which was supposed to be haunted. It was a big, single-storey old farmhouse with dark woodwork and creaky floorboards. We didn't see any ghosts but I was glad to get back into the open daylight and take a walk around its grounds instead.

In the bush we could see a 'mob' of kangaroos, so we set off in pursuit. We managed to get quite close and saw one giant buck, who kept a watchful eye on us while his companions bounced away. As they all hopped off, we started walking in a different direction. Then, out of the corner of my eye, I saw that the giant buck had come after us and was standing up on his hind legs, watching us from about ten feet away.

Lisa was carrying her daughter and, for a moment, I thought the buck was going to charge us and go for Eva. But as we hastened our pace, he turned and sprang back to his pack.

"Bit scary, eh?" I said, as Lisa's eyes met mine, and we got the hell out of there.

Later that day we went to meet Lisa's friend Fiona, who, as well as playing one of Paul Robinson's wives in *Neighbours* a few years earlier, was now heavily involved with animal welfare. Fiona had a houseful of cats, dogs, ducks and chickens and she told us about a friend of hers who had an animal recovery centre. She offered to take me there and I hoped to be able to accept her offer when I returned to Melbourne for my house-sit.

HORIZONS UNLIMITED

Before I left home, several people had asked me if I was going to keep a journal or write a blog (web log) while I was away. Although I intended to keep a journal, I had no intention of doing a blog. I didn't want the hassle of having to update it all the time and besides, I wasn't really sure that anyone would read it.

However, by the time I left home more and more people were asking if I'd do one and then, when I arrived in Australia, Lisa and Lou started asking too. It seemed there might be a large enough audience to make it worthwhile after all.

I applied to Horizons Unlimited for one on their site. Horizons Unlimited is a website dedicated to adventure motorcycling and, as well as hosting blogs, it has all sorts of information and forums about different aspects of motorcycle touring. As well as enquiring about the Oodnadatta Track, I'd found a lot of useful information there about shipping bikes from the UK to Australia.

It took a week or so for the blog to be set up, but it was ready to go just before I was due to leave. I managed to post a few entries before I left Melbourne, which immediately prompted a series of emails from friends back home. These lifted my spirits and encouraged me to keep updating it.

Each entry had to have a title – something I would find myself spending hours contemplating over the coming months. As each day's events unfolded, I'd take ages trying to think up clever or amusing titles to summarise what had happened. It turned out to be one of the most fun aspects of the trip, especially when I was in the saddle most of the day and had little else to do.

RED TAPE AND YELLOW PERIL

After a week of bureaucratic shenanigans, I finally got the bike on Wednesday 22 September – and it was perfect. All it needed was a top box, so the lovely people at Raceway Suzuki found a good secondhand Givi one for me and ordered up the mountings to fix it to the frame. It was anticipated that these would arrive the following day, so it was looking as if I'd be able to get on the road by Friday.

As soon as I got the bike, I took it for an inaugural ride and it ran like a dream. It felt light, held the road well and, now that they'd replaced the exhaust with a quieter one, sped along like a big yellow stealth bomber. Although I liked the name Yellow Peril, I decided just to call it "Yellow", as "Peril" seemed like it could prove a bit predictive. However, even though it was unmistakably yellow, "Yellow" didn't seem to fit either and, in the end, I just called it "the bike".

Lou showed me how to get out of Melbourne, then left me to my own devices. I had a bit of a ride around the local countryside, then realised I hadn't really been paying much attention to the route we'd taken on the way out. Now that I was on my own, I didn't really know the way back. Fortunately, Lisa and I had gone the same way a few days earlier when we went to the Homestead, and I was also in the same area as the Moto Guzzi run, so I knew that if I could find my way back to the Calder Freeway then I'd be able to find my way from there. A quick stop in a small town ascertained the route to the Calder and, as I joined it, I started to recognise landmarks.

As I came into the outskirts of the city, the Calder merged with the Tullamarine Freeway (the road to the airport) and I had a sudden panic as it expanded into a multi-lane motorway with exits to all sorts of places. I couldn't remember if we'd taken the Western Ring. The junction seemed familiar, but did we actually take it? I was past it before I could decide what to do and, as I clocked a row of billboards I'd seen coming back from the airport, I knew I was on the right road.

Now I just needed to find the right exit. Didn't it have a funny set of lanes to cross? God, there it is, I thought, as I got swept along by the stream of traffic. Indicator on.

Now, which lane do I need? Let's go for the outside one. A quick look to see if the lane was free and over I went. Miraculously it spat me out at exactly the right place. A couple of right-handers later and I was back in the safety of Lisa and Lou's front driveway.

I had survived my first solo ride on my new bike. This was going to be a doddle, wasn't it?

RUNS

For several days, I'd been suffering from an attack of the runs. They seemed to be of the nocturnal variety and the night before I was due to get the top box fitted I had a particularly bad dose. Consequently, I wasn't eating very much and by the time I was supposed to take the bike in, I was feeling quite shaky. After several cups of tea and some light-hearted conversation with Lisa, I felt well enough to make the trip.

By the time I got home again, I was feeling considerably better and it occurred to me that perhaps I was more nervous about the trip than I had cared to admit and that my body was expressing its true feelings about how I felt.

I was shitting myself.

Chapter 5: Fear and Loathing in Southern Australia

THE GREAT OCEAN ROAD

By Friday 24 September 2010, I was finally ready to go. Lou lubed my chain, changed my brake fluid and checked my tyres for me before I strapped my vast mound of luggage onto the back seat. I had left the wheelie case behind and was now wearing my bike gear, so I'd been able to repack my clothes into the bike-gear bag. My sleeping bag and the stuff in my backpack I split between a roll-bag I'd brought with me and the top box. I was half-expecting the bike to feel very top- heavy with this configuration, but, as I kicked it into gear and rolled out of Lisa and Lou's driveway, it felt surprisingly stable.

I was excited to be getting on the road, but nervous about riding the new bike and all the weight it was carrying. I'd become a bit of a fair-weather rider since the trip to Finland and every time I did go out on the bike I noticed I wasn't quite as confident as I had been.

A cautious right-hander at the end of the drive and I was on the street. Up a couple of gears and I was approaching the junction with the main road. Back down into first, a touch on the brakes and I came to a stop. Streams of traffic flowed past me, then a gap, out with the clutch and left into the flow. I needed to be in the right-hand lane to get onto the freeway, so a quick look in my mirrors, indicator on, and I was over.

Phew. All was well so far. Up to the lights and a short stop, then back into gear and I was off, down the slip-road onto the freeway.

Christ, there was a lot of traffic. Another look in my mirrors and, "Jesus, look out for that truck!" a strange voice inside my head screamed. "Slow down, let it pass. Now! Pull out, pull out!" It was like a nervous passenger, critiquing my every move. "You need to be quicker than that, you know." Who was this person?

First stop was the bike shop, to see if they had found the spare key to my top box yet. A quick rummage around the back office soon established that they hadn't. This was about the sixth time I'd been in there in two weeks, so they were getting to know me and my plans quite well.

The owner gave me a few pointers on places to visit and they all waved me off as I goose-stepped a straightened leg over the seat and hopped up and down to slide it between the tank and the bags (there wasn't enough space for me to bend my knee and mount the bike normally).

Back onto the freeway and this time I was really on my way. It was a complicated route, which involved riding a short section on the Calder Freeway, then joining the Western Ring Road before merging with the Princes Freeway south. I didn't have Sat Nav or even a map handy, so I had to navigate my way using a combination of guesswork and memory. (Lou had taken me this way to see the Moto Guzzi that was for sale and also six years earlier when we'd gone along the Great Ocean Road.) The traffic was quite heavy, but in the relatively sheltered outskirts of the city I found, much to my relief, that I was handling the bike reasonably well.

Unfortunately, once I got onto the Princes Freeway, the buildings thinned and the road became much more exposed. It was an overcast day with strong winds which buffeted me from one side of the lane to the other. "Christ, hold it steady," the voice in my head kept yelling, every time I got hit by a gust.

It was hard going so, after an hour, I stopped at a service station for fuel and lunch and to gather my composure. As I was scoffing down my all-day breakfast, a truck driver leant over and said, "How d'you like your helmet?"

I had a white flip-face one that was quite popular in the UK but, it would seem, not so common in Australia.

"It's great," I said, immediately feeling better for having someone to talk to.

From there, I successfully managed to navigate my way to Geelong, a large industrial town about 70 or 80 km south-west of Melbourne. After that, I had to pick my way through a series of roadworks and secondary roads to Torquay, where the Great Ocean Road begins.

As I was going along a fairly straight, unremarkable piece of road, a small truck passed me in the opposite direction and suddenly, *wham* – I was almost blown off the road.

"Jesus Christ," the voice shrieked, as I heaved the bike back from the edge of the carriageway. "That was close."

People had warned me about the tailwinds generated by oncoming road trains (trucks pulling three or four trailers), but it came as a real surprise that such a small vehicle could have this effect on me.

When I got to Torquay I thought I would stop and watch the surfers ride the waves for a bit. Torquay is a big surfing town and even in the cold, winter months a hardcore group of them still go out and brave the elements.

Now, you'd think pulling over would be a relatively simple manoeuvre, but as I approached the kerb I encountered my first real problem with riding on Australian roads – adverse cambers. Most of the roads outside the cities have a huge camber, so the outside edge of the road can be several inches lower than it is in the middle of the lane. This means that if you have to stop, your left foot is lower than your right and the bike, of course, leans to that side. This is not a problem if you're unladen, but when you're carrying the equivalent of another person on the back, getting the bike upright again can require the weight-lifting abilities of an Olympic athlete.

Not possessing such abilities, I couldn't park parallel to the kerb, as putting the bike on the side stand would lean it so far over to the left that I'd need a tractor to get it level again. Instead, I had to swing the bike round and reverse it into the space at an angle. Again, not a problem if you're unladen, but manoeuvring a big, heavy machine over such a surface isn't easy and I had to ride back and forth several times before I found a space I could ride in and out of easily.

Leaving Torquay, I joined the Great Ocean Road. There was a signpost at the side of the road headed "THE GREAT OCEAN ROAD", with the distances to various destinations listed below. It was my first milestone so I wanted to get a photo of it to mark the occasion. I pulled over to the side and quickly discovered my next problem with Aussie roads – gravel. Unlike in Britain, Australian roads don't taper into a nice sealed edge; they turn into rough, gravel surfaces. Stopping a bike on a sealed surface is one thing – the tyres grip firmly and you can usually come to a smooth, controlled stop – but stopping on gravel, especially if you misjudge the amount of braking required, can produce a Chernobyl-like plume of dust and a wheel spin that skids the back end off to one side like a frisbee in flight.

Managing to avoid the frisbee effect on this occasion, I dismounted and snapped happily for a few minutes. I'd only come about 100 km but it felt like my trip was now well and truly underway and put me in much better spirits.

Off the freeway system, the traffic eased and it turned into a fabulous ride. No wonder it's considered one of the world's classic bike rides – lots of long, sweeping bends, steep cliffs dropping off just feet from the edge of the road and fantastic views of the ocean and surrounding scenery. I would have loved to stop and take more photos but all the lay-bys were made of gravel, providing far too many unwelcome opportunities to practise my skid recovery techniques, so I just kept going.

I started to relax as I got into the rhythm of going back and forth through the bends and taking in the views of bush-covered hillsides making their way down to sandy beaches and rocky coves. Pretty little holiday homes speckled the slopes, interspersed with the odd spectacular luxury residence. Sea inlets were spanned by small bridges as the road made its way down to the water's edge. The smell of eucalyptus filled the air as the road wound back up through tall forests of gum trees, only to be replaced by the scent of sea salt on the way back down again.

I could feel myself becoming quite mesmerised by it all and was rudely awoken when another biker suddenly came hurtling round a bend on the wrong side of the road and almost went straight into me. *Shit*, I thought, as I tried to pull the bike into the left as he pulled his into the right. I held my breath as we whistled passed each other with just a whisker between us. It shocked me out of my reverie and left my heart racing for miles after.

By 4 pm I'd made it to Apollo Bay, a small town right by the sea. I filled up the tank and, as I was starting to lose my concentration and, to some degree, control of the bike, I went in search of the youth hostel (YHA) to book in for the night.

I parked the bike on the road outside, as it was a good solid tarmac surface. But when I checked in, the warden suggested I might want to park it in one of the spaces outside my room, so I didn't have to carry my luggage so far. A kind and reasonable suggestion, one might think, but, as the driveway was made out of compressed sand, it immediately put me on edge. Taking my huge ride over such an uneven surface at the end of a long, tiring day was not something I wanted to do. But it did make sense, so I reluctantly got back on the bike and, just to be on the safe side, used my feet to paddle it up the drive.

APOLLO LANDINGS

After my first real run of any distance (203.7 km), I found I was exhausted, so I decided to land at Apollo Bay for three days. Now I know 200 km isn't that far, but when you're in a foreign country, riding a heavily laden motorcycle in very windy, freezing cold conditions, not having ridden much for two years, and by yourself, it all seems to heighten your anxiety levels, which makes it all the more demanding.

As I got out of bed the next morning, my legs were like lumps of clay. I dragged them to the toilet but they were aching with tiredness. I couldn't figure out why this was. I mean, it's not like they'd been doing very much, just sitting there really. But somehow or other, my legs were giving me a clear message that they weren't up for a repeat performance, so I contented myself with short walks around the town and along the beach, watching the waves swell and crash for hours on end.

Wandering along the sea front, I found a small bookshop with a good section on travel writing. There was an interesting-looking book called *Birdsville*, about a Sydney journalist, Evan McHugh, and his wife, who'd given up their city life for a year and moved to the remote outback town of Birdsville. Intrigued, and in need of something good to read, I bought it.

As time went by the weather started to pick up, and I even got beautiful sunshine for my last day, as I sat on the beach reading my book. The morning I was leaving, though, it was foggy and pouring with rain. But I felt I really should press on so I quickly loaded up the bike and hopped my leg over the saddle.

As soon as I pulled away, my luggage lurched sideways and I had to do an emergency stop before the whole lot came crashing to the ground. In my haste I hadn't secured my bungees very well, causing my load to shift as soon as I started moving. Ten minutes of re-stacking and strapping everything firmly into position in the pouring rain and I was soaking wet – not a good start to the day. Back onto the bike and I pulled off again. This time my load held fast and I paddled my way back down the driveway and onto the road.

As I approached the junction with the highway, which was also the main street (highways in Australia tend to be single-lane roads, similar to A roads in the UK), I came to a wobbling stop. I was nervous this morning, I noticed – more nervous than I'd been on leaving Melbourne.

A faltering right-hander and I was back on the main drag, leaving Apollo Bay behind me. Fortunately, the rain dried up within a few miles, leaving me with just the biting wind and wet road surfaces to contend with.

"Okay, careful now," the voice inside my head said at every bend and, dropping a gear, I'd comply.

The warden at the hostel had told me to turn off the road at Cape Otway if I wanted to see some koalas. Just as I was wondering how far I'd have to go before I saw any, I spotted a large group of Japanese tourists pointing wildly at the trees and enthusiastically taking pictures. This has to be the spot, I thought. I dismounted and soon found myself being drawn into the animated photo-taking of my Japanese companions.

I'd never seen a koala before and was thrilled at the sight of a whole group of them lazing around in the branches above us. At first they looked like strange dark blobs, but then they'd move and you'd realise they were living creatures. They moved slowly and would stretch out an arm in a leisurely manner and pick some leaves off the branches around them. One of them even had a baby cuddled onto its back. It was lovely to see them and I couldn't help but turn to the Japanese tourist next to me and share a big smile.

"Nice bike," he said.

"Thanks," I replied.

"Where you going?"

"Round Australia."

"Wow, that's so cool. Where have you been?"

I told him this was my second day on the road but that I'd be here for a year. He smiled wistfully and we chatted some more. It was a sweet moment and when I got back on the bike I found I was feeling more relaxed. This was the second time that contact with another human being had helped to dissolve my anxiety.

The road crept inwards after that, through more tall eucalyptus forests. The smell was intoxicating and, if I'd had a cold, I'm sure my sinuses would have been cleared in no time.

I had cars ahead of me and cars behind me as the road became more twisting, with numerous hairpin bends. Road signs would indicate the sharpness of the bends with a speed limit stuck under the bend symbol. Most of them were 25 km/h or 35 km/h and I remembered Rod's words when we drove down to Sydney from Cairns on my first trip to Australia. "They give a speed limit for a reason, Jill. If it's 25 km/h it's because it's really sharp."

I seemed to be the only one who knew this rule though, and the car behind me would almost smash into my rear end every time I dropped a gear and engine-braked my way through the turn. My clutch hand was getting tired from constantly shifting between gears. Surely there was a better way to handle the bends than this?

I stopped at a small township called Laver's Hill and had a traditional Aussie Beef Pie. Australia is famous for its meat pies and, according to my *Birdsville* book, there is quite a bit of competition between bakeries to see who can produce the best quality and most unusual flavours. Sadly, this tradition was not evident in Laver's Hill and as I made my way back to the bike I had to do a quick U-turn and pay an emergency visit to the Ladies' Room, as the pie rather rapidly restarted my now stalled digestive track.

System cleansed, I continued on to Port Campbell National Park, where the Twelve Apostles are. These are giant sandstone stacks that were formed by millions of years of erosion of the sandstone coast of which they were formerly a part. A fellow visitor advised me that a few of them had fallen over in the last few years, but it didn't look any different from when I was first there in 1992.

Although the Twelve Apostles are the most famous part, the National Park extends for many miles beyond them, so I spent the next couple of hours riding from one viewpoint to another, hopping on and off the bike, exploring every twist and turn. There were deep gorges and caves as well as more enormous sandstone stacks. Huge, angry waves pounded against them. It was a magnificent place, but the freezing winds made it difficult to enjoy it fully.

It was mid-afternoon by the time I left Port Campbell and I still had a long way to go to my next stop, Port Fairy. As I went inland, the country became very green and lush and was full of picturesque dairy farms. The coastal parts of the Great Ocean Road had plenty of passing places you could pull into to let following traffic go by, but this part didn't have any and I was conscious of struggling to keep up with the speed limit and causing a bit of a tailback.

"For God's sake, it's 100 km/h and you're only at 80," my internal critic would nag, but I was finding the weight of my luggage difficult to handle and didn't dare go any faster.

I needed petrol, too, but finding a suitable petrol station was easier said than done. Oh, there were plenty of them – it was just that I couldn't use them. In the towns and cities, there is usually a deep concrete gutter separating the main carriageway from any shops, driveways or service stations. This means that whenever you need to fill up with fuel you have to negotiate a treacherous dip on the way in and out of the petrol station. Additionally, in the country areas, the forecourts of petrol stations aren't usually sealed, so you have to deal with gravel surfaces. In the worst-case scenario, you have to turn off a steep camber into a deep gutter, ride onto a gravel forecourt to refuel, then cross the gravel again and sink into the gutter before climbing back out the other side to rejoin the main carriageway.

It seemed that every petrol station I passed had one or more of these features and, not wanting to put myself at unnecessary risk, I just rode on by in the hopes of finding a flat, sealed forecourt soon. By the time I found one that met my exacting criteria, just outside Warrnambool, I was starting to shake with hunger, as it had been hours now since the pie at Laver's Hill and a somewhat modest breakfast at Apollo Bay. A couple of chocolate bars and a bottle of water later and I was back on my way.

When I got to Warrnambool, I was obviously starting to tire as, at a set of traffic lights, I almost dropped the bike. A car ahead of me tried to run a red light, thought better of it, slammed on the brakes and reversed back behind the line. All of this I saw, and gave him plenty of space to manoeuvre, but I must have lost my concentration for a moment, as the next thing I knew, I was ripping my arm out of its socket trying to stop the bike from hitting the deck.

Jesus, I thought as I tried to pull it back up again. I had a queue of cars behind me and the last thing I wanted to do was drop the bike and cause a hold-up.

"Come on," I pleaded as I hauled at the handlebars. "Come on." For a moment, I thought I was going to lose it. "Shit!" Then, with one almighty heave, it came back up. "Oh my God!" My heart was pounding and I could feel myself break out in a sweat. "You moron," I berated myself as I kicked it back into gear and moved off.

"What the hell happened there?" the voice demanded for the last 30 km into Port Fairy.

I was shaking and starting to feel weak. It had been a long day (a 210.6 km ride over eight hours) and by the time I reached the youth hostel I was, again, exhausted, so I decided to stay there a couple of nights.

When I checked in, the warden, clearly mistaking me for someone who knew how to handle a heavily overloaded motorcycle, suggested I parked round the back, where I could more easily transfer my luggage to my room. I'd already carefully parked the bike on the street outside the front entrance but, not wanting to offend, I remounted and made my way to the said spot.

The place she'd recommended was a small patch of grass about the same size as the bike, sandwiched between a garage door and a fence. Consequently I couldn't ride straight onto it: I had to do three right-hand turns in a very small car park and then paddle it in. Having achieved this minor feat, I realised I was facing the wrong way to get back out again, so I had to do the equivalent of a three-point turn to rotate it and reverse it into the spot. The side stand then sank into the wet grass and I had a mad panic trying to dig out the hard plastic disc Minna-Ella had given me a few years earlier from my top box, and stick it under the stand before the whole thing passed its tipping point and ploughed into the ground.

That little favour had taken about half an hour and left me stressed out of my box. Why hadn't I just left it round the front?

FAIRY STORIES

The next day I did some exploring. I went round Gilbert's Island, a small, flat nature reserve attached to the mainland by a man-made causeway. In the space of an hour I got soaked by rain, lashed by hail, blown dry by the wind and warmed by a sudden outbreak of sunshine. On the way back, I passed the wharf, where a boatful of fishermen invited me to come on board. Having nothing else in particular to do, I decided I would.

They were hilarious and quite drunk and, when they heard I'd worked on a prawn trawler during my first visit to Oz, offered me a job as a "deckie".

When Lisa and I had got the jobs in Darwin, we were over the moon. We rushed back to the hostel, packed our gear and raced back to the docks to join the trawler. There were five of us on board – the skipper, John, the mate, Al, another deckhand, a Swedish girl called Susie and the two of us. Lisa and I were to be deckhands and I was also going to be the cook, having had a season as a chalet girl the previous year. Motoring out from Darwin harbour that night was one of the most blissful moments of my life. The sun was setting, painting the sky a radiant crimson, and out of nowhere, a school of dolphins appeared alongside the stern of the boat and jumped through the waves beside us for a while.

I wish I could say the rest of the trip was as magical, but it turned out that prawn trawling was a terribly destructive form of fishing. Huge nets are dragged along the ocean floor, uprooting anything in their path. The mesh of the nets is quite small, so all sorts of things get trapped in them. We caught sharks, sting rays and turtles, as well as all manner of fish and crustaceans. The nets were emptied onto a tray and the catch was shovelled down a chute onto a conveyor belt, where we would pick out the prawns from the other creatures, which were returned to the sea. Unfortunately, by the time most of them got back to the water, they were dead.

Prawn trawling is done at night, as the prawns sink to the bottom when they sleep, so we had to get up four or five times during the night to bring in each catch. I usually managed to make it up for the first couple of catches, but after that I'd be almost comatose and Lisa would have to shake me awake time after time, before I staggered out of bed and onto the deck. Had I known what I was getting into before I started, I would never have done it.

We crossed the Gulf of Carpentaria and went round Cape York, the northern tip of Australia, where we had to deal with massive sixteen-metre swells. Anything that wasn't tied down would get thrown from one side of the boat to the other and, being on the top bunk, I almost got thrown out of bed several times. It was a gruelling experience.

So, despite being flattered by my new friends' offer, this time I wasn't so keen. Upon further enquiry it turned out they fished for shark and cray (lobster) and went out for five days at a time. As the boat was not in the finest condition and I was pretty sure that being a deckie would involve having to kill the catch when it arrived on deck – not to mention that the skipper, nice as he was, had two black eyes – I decided to decline their kind offer.

To make up for the priceless experience I'd no doubt be missing out on, one of the others then offered me the skipper's hand in marriage. Again, I politely declined.

FLOUTING THE LAW

I left Port Fairy the next day. It had been a fun visit – nice people at the hostel and a disastrous attempt to French plait an English girl's hair (I warned her I couldn't do it).

It was a huge ride, 314.3 km, to my next port of call, Robe. It took me two hours to do the first 130 km, but what a fabulous ride. One of the women at the hostel, Barbara, told me about a back road that I could take to Nelson and on to Mount Gambier. It started where the Great Ocean Road seemed to run out at Portland, and went up through acres of pine plantations.

There was hardly another soul on the road and I was able to beetle along at my own pace and take in all the sights and sounds. Occasionally there would be a break in the forest, which gave way to spectacular views of the coastline below. It was cool and reasonably sheltered so I got a bit of relief from the constant winds and, despite a warning from Barbara to look out for hordes of logging trucks which would "blow me off the road if I wasn't careful", I passed only a few, which were all going along at a fairly sedate pace.

I had a stop in Nelson, a small town located at the mouth of a river. I pulled up in the car park and spent a few minutes watching the kids paddle about in canoes and the men fish from the jetty. Then a genial retired couple pulled in and started chatting. I explained I was planning to rejoin the Princes Highway at Mount Gambier and take it round to Robe.

The man frowned at this and said, "I'm not sure you can do that." He fished out his road atlas, since I only had a giant map of Australia, which didn't show enough detail, and I saw that the Princes Highway, indeed, did not go past Robe and that I'd need to take another secondary road, the Southern Ports Highway, after the town of Millicent instead.

Hmm, maybe I should get myself a decent road atlas, I thought as I headed off. I'd started to realise that a wrong turn in Australia could add hundreds of kilometres onto a journey and, as I was already feeling the strain of being in the saddle for so long (my bum was aching and my accelerator hand was cramping badly), I didn't want to end up off course too often.

The road was going inland now and I crossed the border from Victoria into South Australia about 10 km before Mount Gambier. You're not allowed to transport fresh fruit or vegetables between states in Australia as it may spread fruit fly, so there was a rather pathetic-looking bin in an unattended lay-by at the side of the road with a sign instructing travellers to deposit their unwanted foodstuffs in it. As it was overflowing and clearly uncared for, I rode past, ignoring the instructions, thinking, *I wonder how many people bother to stop at these places and get rid of their fruit?*

A few kilometres later, I rounded a corner and ran into a huge Customs area, where I was flagged down. Apparently they take their fruit fly control very seriously in South Australia and have the power to confiscate goods and fine offenders heavily if they haven't complied. My heart sank as I tried to remember if I had any food on board.

A quick examination by a (thankfully) friendly customs inspector revealed that I was fruit-free, but I slunk off after my inspection feeling somewhat guilty for having entertained the thought of disobeying such "trivial" rules.

I had a navigational breakdown in Mount Gambier, where I wanted to stop and see the Blue Lake, which was formed in the crater of an extinct volcano. On approaching the town, I could see a hill off to my left, which, had my logic circuits been working, would have given me a clue as to where the crater was. But my logic circuits were out to lunch and instead of following the road up the hill, I decided to follow it into town. *Funny, no sign of a lake here.*

On through the centre of town and out the other side. You'd think I'd have realised I was going in the wrong direction by now, but no, logic had completed its starter and was well into its main course, so I carried on riding. The land had become flat by this time. Ah-ha, logic had finished dessert and was back on the job. "This isn't right – turn round, you idiot, and go back."

But where to turn? It was a busy main highway. Then I spied a timber yard to my left. Despite a sign saying "No Unauthorised Vehicles", it was my best bet, so I executed what has to be the widest U-turn ever undertaken and made my way back across the highway and through the town. Logic, feeling somewhat buoyed by its hearty lunch, assisted with the navigation this time and quickly had us back on track. Up the hill, then left into a clearly signposted street. Left again and I was there.

Another parking fiasco quickly followed. There were spaces all around but all of them tapered into deep gutters requiring tricky manoeuvres to get the bike parked safely.

When I finally managed to dismount and walked over to the viewpoint, I was somewhat disappointed to see that the lake wasn't that blue at all. Apparently, there are certain times of the year when a particular type of algae makes it a deep turquoise blue, but unfortunately this was not one of them.

Leaving the town, I retraced my steps down the hill and back past the timber yard before picking up the Southern Ports Highway to Robe. The sun had come out now, lifting my spirits. As there was hardly any traffic, I made good time – even finding myself at 100 km/h on some stretches.

I had another stop at a gorgeous seaside town called Beachport, which had beautiful turquoise blue waters and a long jetty stretching far into the sea. I walked to the end of the jetty and stared into the alluring waters, the bitter wind helping me resist the temptation of diving in.

Then I started the last section to Robe. I was at sea level now and the road was very exposed. The clear blue skies and sunshine fooled me into thinking this would be an enjoyable stretch, but as I proceeded through a patchwork of sandy sea lakes on one side and empty farmland on the other, one powerful gust of wind after another smashed into me, throwing me from one side of the carriageway to the other and leaving my nerves in tatters. I'm sure there must be an official technique for riding in such conditions, but I didn't know what it was.

The trouble with gusting wind is that you never know when the next gust is coming. If it's a steady crosswind you can lean the bike into it, but when it's gusting you just have to do your best to steer back to your side of the road once it stops. Hugging the nearside as tightly as I could seemed like the best way to avoid getting blown into the path of an oncoming truck.

I eventually rolled into Robe at 4 pm, tired and very shaken.

As if I wasn't having enough trouble with parking spaces already, after I'd spent fifteen minutes parking the bike on soggy, wet earth at the front of the youth hostel, the warden appeared and, once again, suggested I could park it round the back.

Oh God, I thought as I flashed back to the previous night's caper at Port Fairy. Did I really want a repeat of that performance? Well, it seemed I did, as I proceeded to paddle the bike up a small ramp at the side of the building onto a paved walkway which led to a small patio at the rear. But, God, I was shaking. These slow manoeuvres with so much weight were really straining my nerves.

TIME IN JAIL

The Robe youth hostel was the former home of an early British settler. It was a single-storey, heavy-set stone building which had a slightly haunted feel to it. It had a massive, long, dark corridor and all the rooms were huge, with great high ceilings and heavy, dark oak doors and windows.

As I was making dinner, a friendly French guy called Luc asked me if I wanted to join him and some others for a video night. I happily accepted and spent the evening watching the *Crocodile Dundee* trilogy in an effort to avoid encountering any ghosts.

The following day, I went off to explore the town. I'd walked to the outskirts of it the day before when I went to buy some food, but the hostel warden told me there was a shortcut I could take over the beach instead.

I set off, as instructed, following a footpath past some houses and over a footbridge. It brought me out on the beach – *so far, so good*. Then I became very disorientated. When I'd ridden into Robe, the sea was on the left, but now it was on the right and, as the town centre was north from the hostel, I couldn't figure out which way to go, now that the sea had mysteriously changed position.

I walked over to some houses, found what seemed like a main road and turned left. I must have walked for about an hour before I saw a road sign indicating that Robe was in the opposite direction. Somehow I'd accidently ended up walking back down the Southern Ports Highway away from the town, rather than towards it. I now had to about-turn and walk back in again. It was only when I told the warden what had happened that I realised that Robe actually lies on a peninsula and that's why the sea had suddenly switched sides.

At the harbour, a fishing boat was unloading its catch of shark. This boat was a lot cleaner, more organised and sober than my friends at Port Fairy. It turned out that the deckies do have to behead and gut the fish, so I was right to refuse the job with the Port Fairy boys, as I wouldn't have wanted killing sharks on my conscience.

The sharks themselves are only about two to three feet long and quite small and skinny but, as a local onlooker informed me, the fishermen use 10 m high nets which are 3–4 km (that's kilometres!) long and drag along the bottom. This means that, even though they have a 6 cm mesh which allows the smaller fish to swim free, they are still quite destructive.

I continued my tour of Robe, which included a visit to the Old Gaol House. This was now a ruin so I wasn't detained too long.

BUGS, BITES & BUNK BEDS

After a day of laundry and motorcycle maintenance (that is to say washing it, lubing the chain and filling up the fuel tank), I rode from Robe to Port Elliot – another 314.2 km journey. The Southern Ports Highway rejoined the Princes Highway at Kingston SE and snaked its way along another long stretch of low-level coastal inlets, battered by more strong winds. The roads were relatively clear but the air was full of insects, presumably brought out by the sunny skies and increase in temperature.

By the time I stopped for lunch in Meningie, I was covered in the little critters. When I went to the loo, one of them must have got caught in my clothing, as when I took my trousers down I got stung about five times on the bum. Having just read about scorpion bites in my *Birdsville* book, I waited for the onset of poison-induced paralysis. But after about ten minutes and no loss of movement, I figured it was probably just a bee, so I got some sting-relieving ointment instead.

Since leaving the Great Ocean Road, I hadn't seen many other bikes. Now though, probably because it was a Saturday, quite a lot of them were on the road. Many of them pulled into the service station at Salt Creek. One even had a trailer attached to it, which the rider informed me made no difference to the handling, although a 1300 cc engine was required to pull it.

As I approached a town called Tailem Bend, I couldn't tell which way to go from my giant map. Since Port Elliott was west, I decided to turn left off the highway and take the road to Wellington. This took me to a small car ferry (or "punt", as the man who loaded me on called it), which plied the traffic across the mighty Murray River all day long.

I've always loved ferry rides – they remind me of childhood trips to Europe, when I always felt that getting the ferry to France was the real start of the holiday. I found myself getting quite excited at the prospect of a little ferry crossing and thoroughly enjoyed the 100 metres or so to the other side.

However, I still wasn't convinced I'd taken the right road, so I stopped at a petrol station to enquire. It turned out the man behind the desk was from Sri Lanka and wasn't familiar with the local geography, but fortunately a local man came in behind me and confirmed that I was, indeed, heading in the right direction.

The road went through an area called the Coorung, which was a mixture of pasturelands and sea inlets and made for a beautiful backdrop.

On arriving at the Port Elliot youth hostel, I found a space to park between two cars and reversed the bike into the gutter tail first. With the nose pointing out at an angle, I put the stand down, dismounted and admired my handiwork. *Yes, that should do the job.*

When I checked in, the warden advised, "There's a car park around the back, if you want to park your bike in there."

Eh? Was I having déjà vu? But I'd wisened up by now. "Er, is it sealed?" I asked.

"No, it's gravel," was the reply.

I thanked him politely and left it exactly where it was for the next three days.

During check-in I was informed that I'd be sharing a room with another girl, but that she'd already claimed the bottom bunk so I'd be on the top one. Now, for a 20-year-old nimble backpacker this is no inconvenience, but for a 47-year-old stiffie like myself it was a major challenge.

It doesn't take a structural engineer to figure out that if you put the equivalent of a flattened whale on top of four lollipop sticks, it is not going to be the most stable structure, so clambering up the tiny set of ladders attached to the side of the beds almost toppled the whole lot. However, I'm glad to report that after a few attempts I perfected the technique and was able to manage the ascent and descent without incident – much to the relief of my roommate.

BREAKING DOWN

Something I hadn't had time to do before I left Melbourne was take out breakdown cover. The bike had been going well and so far I'd been in fairly populated areas, but I knew that if I ended up in more remote parts of the country, I'd be completely screwed if the bike broke down. I hadn't the first idea how to do repairs. I couldn't even point out where the carburettor was, if it even had one, that is. I knew how to check the oil, top up the brake fluid, lube the chain, inflate the tyres and put petrol in it, but other than that I was a complete airhead when it came to mechanics.

I'd meant to organise cover after I left Melbourne, but by the time I got to where I was going each day, I had completely forgotten. So it wasn't until I arrived in Port Elliot that I finally remembered to do it. The lady from the Royal Automobile Club of Victoria (RACV) was extremely helpful and very interested in my trip. She seemed fascinated that I was not only doing it on a motorcycle but that I was doing it by myself. She even took down the details of my blog and promised to follow how I got on. I was really touched by this and very glad that I'd finally made the call.

WHALE WATCHING AND SEAL SPOTTING

Once again, I was exhausted by my long ride, so I decided to spend a couple of days in Port Elliot. The first day, I didn't make it much further than the village shops and the nearest beach, but the next one I thought I spotted a whale from the hostel balcony so I went charging over the headland to see if I could capture some photos of it.

As I approached, I realised that the mass I'd spotted from the hostel wasn't moving or changing shape. Upon closer inspection, it turned out it was actually a large rock. Just as I was dejectedly putting my camera away, a family with a huge number of children arrived on the scene and pointed out where a real whale was. *Hoorah, I saw a whale!* However, it was a bit too far away to make out any detail.

On the way back, I decided to take advantage of the gorgeous South Australian sunshine that was now making an appearance, and paddled along the beach. As I was putting my shoes back on at the end of it, I thought I saw some seals by the jetty. Once again I raced round the bay, only to discover it was three guys in wetsuits and snorkels. So maybe my wildlife-spotting skills needed some improvement, but I was definitely not short of enthusiasm.

That night I went to the pub with my roommate, Paula. We'd been having a bit of a laugh sharing together, so it was good to get to know her better. She was in her early thirties, lived in Adelaide and had just come down to the Coorung for a few days' holiday. We passed the night away bemoaning the state of our love lives and the various disastrous attempts friends and family had made to assist us in finding men.

She was really fun and when she suggested that I look her up if I passed through Adelaide, I made the mistake of letting my bike fear get the better of me and didn't take her details. Given how much trouble I was having handling the bike on quiet country roads, I had no desire to go anywhere near a big, busy city. It was a decision I was later to regret.

Chapter 6: Confidence Crisis

LOSING CONTROL

Paula came down to wave me off the following morning. I gave her my *Birdsville* book, which I'd now finished, and rode the 60-odd km along the Fleurieu Penninsula to Cape Jervis, from where I'd be able to catch the ferry to Kangaroo Island. I was feeling nervous again – what with the winds, the rain, the bends, the parking dramas, the near misses and almost dropping the bike, it seemed like practically every day I'd had some sort of close call, and my confidence had taken a bit of a pounding.

As I left the hostel, the voice was back. "Careful now, don't want to drop it in the turn, better to be safe than sorry ...", so I paddled the bike into a straight line before pulling off and wobbling my way down the road. At the end of the street, where I had to do a left turn onto the main highway, I swung out way too wide and ended up on the wrong side of the road. "Jesus, you're riding like a complete beginner," the judge inside my head criticised again.

I had hoped to stop in a town called Victor Harbour, which had an interesting wooden jetty that curved around a hilly outcrop, but I couldn't find anywhere to park that didn't involve paying money or parking on an adverse camber, so I kept riding. As I was leaving the town I came to a roundabout on a hill, with an extreme camber on the left. A car was approaching from the right but I knew that if I stopped I'd almost certainly go over, as my left foot would be a lot lower than my right one, and that everything would lurch so heavily to the left that I'd have difficulty holding the bike upright. So I opened up the throttle and raced out in front of it. I knew the driver had to hit the brakes to avoid me, but I just kept going, as another near drop was the last thing I wanted.

The weather had been quite mild when I left Port Elliot, so I'd put on my new summer riding gloves, but as I climbed up into more forests, the temperature dropped. After a while, my fingers were numb and I knew I'd have to pull over and change back to my winter gloves, but I couldn't find anywhere to stop. Every junction, lay-by or siding was gravel and, as I was already feeling pretty jumpy, I didn't want to risk pulling onto it and skidding. Eventually I found a piece of road with a six-inch narrow strip of tarmac at the side, where I was able to stop and make the change.

I got back on the bike and continued, soon joining the road to Cape Jervis. This involved a steep descent down a narrow, twisty road – and I now had two tour buses behind me. I tried to keep up a decent speed on the straights but I was useless on the bends, dropping down to 30 or 40 km/h and causing endless annoyance behind me.

When I finally made it into the car park at the ferry terminal, I slammed on the brakes so hard that the bike jerked to another violent stop.

"Jesus Christ, Jill, what the hell are you doing?" I berated myself. I was really starting to lose control.

KANGAROO ISLAND

It was a gorgeous, sunny crossing over to Kangaroo Island (or KI, as it's known locally) and I even spotted a baby dolphin leaping through the waves.

Coming into Penneshaw, the main town on this part of the island, I could see a beautiful white, sandy beach surrounded by clear, glistening, turquoise waters. It hadn't been a long day's ride, but getting off the ferry I was a nervous wreck.

The deckhands helped me untie the bike, but riding it down the ramp and onto the quayside saw me practically paddle it all the way there. I knew I wasn't doing myself any favours by being so over-cautious every time I had to cross an uneven surface and that undertaking manoeuvres at a higher speed would make things easier, but I just couldn't get myself to do it. I was terrified of dropping the bike, and going ridiculously slowly was the only way I trusted myself to avoid it. I was losing my nerve.

Despite Penneshaw being a very small town, I managed to take the wrong road, missed the youth hostel and ended up riding right out of town and past the beach. I didn't feel up to doing a U-turn, so I had to go up a hill, turn left past a row of houses, then left again back down the hill, before doing a final left-hander back onto the main road. An absurd detour for what could have been a simple U-turn, had I not got a tonne of luggage on the back, undermining my confidence.

As I was now approaching from the opposite direction, I spotted the youth hostel this time, only to find it had a gravel car park. *Oh no*, I thought as I pulled in.

I spent the next twenty minutes paddling my way back and forth, trying to park the bike in such a way that I could get it back out again. Christ, I wasn't handling the bike at all well.

Having installed myself in my room, I went off on foot to have a look around. The sea was crystal clear and I spent the rest of the afternoon walking along the beach, trying to wash away my fears.

The next morning, I set off to explore the rest of the island. I needed fuel, so I stopped in the small township of American River, where the general store had a single pump outside.

Another biker rode up as I was pulling away and I stopped to speak to him. His name was Croley Graham (which struck me as odd; I thought it should be Graham Croley). He'd flown his bike over from America and was finishing off a tour of the western half of Australia, which had taken just over six weeks. Six weeks to ride round the western half of Oz seemed like an incredibly short period of time to me, but obviously he was covering a lot more ground each day than I was – a feat no doubt assisted by having a big BMW adventure touring bike, neat metal panniers and just a small yellow tent strapped to his back seat.

As we were talking, a storm blew up out of nowhere and threw sand and rain everywhere. After that, the wind didn't stop all day, so it was a tough ride. I got as far as Seal Bay, where I saw some sea lions, and then decided to head back.

KI is quite a big island (150 km long and 50 km wide), with only two main roads. You have to travel about 50 km from Penneshaw before you get to the point where the road splits, so, as I was freezing and knackered, a trip a quarter of the way along the southern route was enough for me.

That night a young French girl arrived at the hostel. She was in a bit of state because she'd had a bad WWOOF (Willing Workers on Organic Farms)[1] experience. She was also separated from her boyfriend and, because the shops had now closed, had nothing to eat. As I'd been a bit worried that I was supposed to pay to see the sea lions and had just marched straight through the Visitor Centre and down to the beach without paying my dues, I was feeling a bit guilty and was looking for a way to settle my suspected karmic debt. I therefore gave her the remainder of my packet of biscuits, cooked her some pasta and let her use my phone to speak to her boyfriend. This seemed to cheer her up enormously and she even managed to organise another WWOOF placement for a few days' time.

The next day, the sun was shining in Penneshaw, but I decided to catch up on some domestic chores (like laundry and having a massage) instead of doing the inland road, as it was bitterly cold and I reckoned the weather wouldn't be too good in the middle of the island. My French friend, who'd taken a bus tour, later confirmed that it had been wild, so I felt I'd made the right decision.

There is a colony of Fairy Penguins in the dunes at Penneshaw. During the day they swim out to sea to fish for their families, so it's rare to see them, but at night they return with their catch and make their way to their burrows on the shore. I'd seen the Fairy Penguins at Phillip Island during a previous visit and they were utterly delightful, so that night I decided to go on the Penguin Tour run by the local Park Rangers. After a short introductory talk they took us out to see them. Much to everyone's surprise, there was one brave penguin guarding the entrance to his nest, right outside the door of the Ranger Station. We'd all been standing next to it without noticing it, until the Ranger pointed it out.

We made our way round the headland, past lots of empty burrows to a viewing platform where suddenly we could hear a cacophony of squawking. As the adult penguins made their way up through the rocks from the shore, the baby ones came out of their burrows and yelled at them to hurry up. There was then a feeding frenzy as the brood fought for the food the parents were transporting. It was charming to watch and I found myself smiling contentedly as the youngsters clambered over each other, occasionally sliding down the slope in an attempt to get their fair share.

It amazes me how nature adapts. These little creatures have no hands, yet they are still able to carry food to their families by stuffing themselves full of fish and then regurgitating it.

NERVOUS WRECKAGE

After leaving Apollo Bay, my bike-handling skills seemed to get progressively worse. Although I'd thought that the mountain of luggage didn't make the bike top-heavy when I left Melbourne, this did not remain the case. I guess that when I left I was on motorways for the first couple of hours and then, after the short stop at Torquay, I pretty much did a continuous ride to Apollo Bay, so I wasn't stopping and starting too much and wasn't so aware of the weight. However, the further I went, the more anxious I got. It started making me jumpy, especially when I had to stop in gravel lay-bys or on rough surfaces. I even had a couple of really bad stops in perfectly flat, sealed car parks.

But after smoothly riding around Kangaroo Island unladen, I realised that the excessive weight had caused me to develop a nasty habit of slamming on the front brake every time I stopped, which was causing the bike to lurch forward and throw everything out of balance. This was the reason I'd nearly dropped the bike in Warrnambool earlier in the week. I'd always been a keen back brake user, but obviously the anxiety was making me panicky and causing me to grab the front brake instead. I needed to be gentler with the front brake and to start using the back brake again, in order to control my stops more smoothly.

I also decided I'd need to get some panniers, which would hopefully lower the centre of gravity and make the handling a bit easier. Otherwise, I was afraid I'd become a nervous wreck and spend the entire trip avoiding uneven surfaces, gravel or adverse cambers. Which, given that virtually everywhere outside the cities falls into this category, meant I wouldn't be going anywhere very much at all.

By the end of my time in KI, I decided to go to Adelaide. Originally I hadn't planned on doing this, as the thought of navigating my way into a major city terrified me, but the need for a better luggage system and the promise of a bit more to do on foot (see, I was looking for ways to avoid riding already) persuaded me it would be a good idea.

I was due to get a mid-morning ferry back from KI to the mainland and I was up and packed bright and early. It was only a few metres from the hostel to the ferry terminal, so I rode round and joined the queue with plenty of time to spare. As I waited, a few bikes joined the queue, including a family split over two bikes. The mother and son were on a Triumph Bonneville SE and the father and daughter were on a large Japanese bike with a home-made trailer emblazoned with Coca-Cola insignia attached to the back. The family as a whole looked as if they had about the same amount of luggage as I did.

I was one of the first to be loaded onto the ferry, so I made my way to the top deck as soon as the bike was secured. As I watched the remaining vehicles board, a man came up and started talking to me. He was a biker too, although he wasn't on his bike on this occasion. But he'd been watching all the bikes and had identified that I'd been on the big yellow one with all the luggage. This is when he made his comment about my load. I know he meant well, but I really needed uplifting at this point, not being brought down, so I went inside and watched an infomercial for a weight loss machine instead.

Watching various lithe models swing from one side to the other on it just made me feel worse. Not only was I scared witless, I was fat as well, and unlikely ever to reclaim the nimble, slender figure of my youth. When the ferry docked at Cape Jervis, I rode off at the other end feeling like shite.

Now I had the steep hill back up to the junction with the Fleurieu Penninsula to tackle. My stomach was knotted and before long I had a huge queue of traffic behind me. I wanted to pull over and let them pass, but all the lay-bys were gravel and I didn't have the nerve to stop.

As the road split and I took the fork to Adelaide, even more traffic started to bear down on me. *Shit, what am I going to do?* This road was incredibly twisty, which meant I couldn't get my speed faster than 40 km/h through the bends and not much over 80 km/h on the straights, and the straights weren't long enough for anyone to overtake. I needed fuel, so a stop in a petrol station would have been the ideal solution, but I couldn't find one anywhere. I was not enjoying this ride.

Finally, I came into a small town called Normanville. *Phew*, I thought – at least I'll be able to pull over here. But there wasn't a petrol station to be seen and all the parking areas had the same extreme camber problem I'd been encountering since leaving Melbourne, so I just had to carry on.

This fear of uneven surfaces was starting to make me a hazard to other road users. "Come on, faster," the voice kept saying, but the faster I tried to go, the more scared I got.

Gradually all the traffic made it past me and I felt highly embarrassed when the biker family overtook me on a bend, waving as they passed. I was not setting a good example.

Eventually, about 20 km from Adelaide, I found a petrol station with a concrete forecourt. Oh, the relief of being able to stop without the fear of skidding to a dusty end.

An hour later, fed and rested, it was time to rejoin the main road into Adelaide. Before long, this single-lane highway turned into a massive three-lane approach road full of cars, trucks, buses and vans. They all seemed to know exactly where they were going and were cutting in and out all around me as they veered off to their various destinations.

My heart was racing and my arms were rigid with tension, but I knew that the type of panicky behaviour I'd been exhibiting earlier wasn't going to help me, so, as I came into the traffic light controlled downtown area, I made a concerted effort to use the back brake whenever I had to stop or slow down, and gradually I started to regain control of the bike.

The hostel warden at Penneshaw had printed off directions to the Adelaide youth hostel for me, but as I had no way of mounting them on the bike or any GPS to guide me, I had to navigate my way from memory. Remarkably, I managed to get to all-but-one street from the hostel before I had to pull over and check the map. Despite the fact that I'd handled the approach quite well, I was so relieved to have made it, I almost dropped to my knees and kissed the tarmac when I pulled up in front of the hostel.

I had survived riding into my first major city. Now it was time to do something about my luggage.

Chapter 7: Doubt

BAGGAGE HANDLING

One of the problems of travelling with such a ridiculously large amount of luggage is transporting it all to and from the bike. In most of the hostels I'd stayed in, I'd been accommodated in ground floor rooms, so although several trips were still involved to load/unload, at least I didn't have to carry the luggage too far. But as the youth hostel in Adelaide was right in the city centre and had parking restrictions outside, I had to unload all my luggage into the foyer, find somewhere to park the bike and then carry all my bags up to the second floor. Granted, there was a lift, but carrying anything in full motorcycle clothing is never easy. Combined with the effects of a stressful ride from KI, I was a heaving, sweaty mess by the end of it.

As soon as I got settled into my room, I went off to the nearest bike shop to get a set of panniers to re-distribute my luggage. There was only one pair that were anything like big enough, so I bought them without a second thought, despite the $200 price tag. They had 35-litre bags on each side, meaning they would take a total of 70 litres worth of stuff, the same as my bike-gear bag. Returning to my room with my new prize, I unpacked everything and started transferring it.

As I was in a repacking frenzy, my new room-mate Lilly arrived and, obviously sensing I was on the verge of a meltdown, took me off to the pub where, a glass of wine later, sanity was restored.

Lilly was a fun lady in her forties who had been a vet but was now doing a creative writing course in an attempt to establish a new career for herself. She lived in northern Victoria and was coming through to Adelaide every month or so to do the course. She had that big, open, Aussie personality that I liked so much, and I instantly took to her. Over the next couple of days, although we went our separate ways during the day, it was a real laugh sharing with her whenever she returned.

JUST WHEN YOU THINK THE WORST IS OVER

The next day I got an email from my brother Chris, saying that his good friends Pete and Susie lived in Adelaide and I should look them up. I did, and they invited me to come and visit them in their home in the Adelaide Hills the following day.

They gave me directions which included the phrase "I hope you don't mind bends?" Just when I thought there could be no bendier a road than the one I'd done coming from KI, I discovered that I was hopelessly mistaken. The road up to their house twisted and turned its way up a steep hillside for about 30 km.

I missed the turn-off to their house, so I phoned Pete, who came and got me. After we'd meandered along a series of pretty village roads, my heart stopped as he led me onto a dirt track. *Oh my God*, I thought. My worst nightmare was about to come true. For a moment, I seriously considered doing a U-turn and getting the hell out of there, but I knew I would probably end up in even worse trouble if I did, so I just followed on.

I don't know why I'd developed such a phobia about gravel roads. I mean, it wasn't as if I hadn't done them before. In Finland, I hadn't given them a second thought, but since I'd been in Australia, I'd got a real thing about them. Clearly, the weight of all my luggage had really shaken my confidence and anything that was going to make it even harder to handle the bike got me very nervous. I couldn't believe I'd actually been thinking about doing the Oodnadatta Track, when I didn't even want to ride up to Pete's house.

After a short distance, Pete turned off the flat dirt road onto a steep driveway. This involved a sharp left-hand turn. Completely losing my nerve, I stopped and used my feet to paddle the bike round the corner. For an instant I thought about leaving it at the bottom and walking up. But this would have involved a serious loss of face so I gulped back my terror, put on the power and skidded my way up the drive.

I screeched to a halt at the top of the hill, where Pete and Susie were now waiting, leaving the aforementioned Chernobyl-like plume of dust behind me, and shakily dismounted. Not the most auspicious way to meet my new friends.

Clearly Chris had never mentioned that he had a sister as Pete and Susie seemed really surprised to learn that I existed. However, they welcomed me into their home and seemed reassured, not to mention amused, to see that I not only bore a strong family resemblance to my brother but also had all the same mannerisms and speech patterns.

I instantly liked Pete and Susie. They were both in their fifties but looked more like a couple of thirty-year-olds. Susie was slim and petite with long blond hair, while Pete was tall and lean. Susie was a fantastic cook, as I discovered when she rustled up some eggs Benedict within a few minutes of my arrival. They had both lived overseas and travelled a lot, so we had plenty in common and I found them really easy to talk to.

After breakfast, they took me off to see some of the sights of the Adelaide Hills. These hills house a number of villages, several of which were built in the style of the people who founded them. For instance, we went to Hahndorf, a German-themed one. It reminded me of a German Christmas market, even though the sun was shining. We also went to visit a local winery, an industry for which the Hills are famed. Finally, they took me to see a giant chocolate factory. We were too late to see any chocolate being made, but a wander round the factory shop provided ample opportunity to sample its wares.

Back at their house, Susie made a fantastic dinner from things we'd purchased throughout the day. They were such fun people and I really appreciated their hospitality.

Getting the bike back down the dirt track when I was leaving was even more scary than getting it up there, and left me pretty shaken. Even though the bike was now unladen, my nerves were still frayed and it seemed I'd left my riding skills somewhere back on the practice pad in Glasgow. As I got back onto the twisty road home, I was going so slowly that even a cyclist overtook me.

"God, get a grip," I kept telling myself, but it was no use, I had no confidence left. I later found out from my brother that Susie had sent him an email saying she was "really worried about me being on that bike".

As I anxiously made my way back to the hostel, I was beginning to think that what I really needed to do was find a nice empty car park somewhere and practise manoeuvres for a day until I got my confidence back.

ADELAIDE

Adelaide was a wonderful city. Four large avenues formed a rectangle around the central business district (CBD), separating it from the suburbs by a wide border of parklands on all sides. The CBD was small enough to walk from one side to the other quite easily, but large enough to accommodate a wide variety of shops, offices, hotels and public spaces. The Torrens River flowed behind the North Terrace and provided a beautiful haven for waterfowl and wildlife.

If I had to find a word to describe Adelaide, I would say "easy". Everything about the city was easy – it was easy to get into, it was easy to get out of, it was easy to get around, it was easy to make friends, it was easy to find what you needed. It was all just so easy. I loved it.

The weather had been heating up, so the first week I spent mostly exploring the city centre and getting my bike sorted out. I still only had one key for the top box, so I thought it would be sensible to get another one cut. I found a locksmith, who advised me, "If that doesn't work, bring it back and I'll make it work." As it happened, it didn't work, so I took it back and, sure enough, he made it work. See, *easy*.

I also noticed, after my ride up into the Adelaide Hills, that my chain was loose, and took it to the bike shop to get it tightened. They informed me that it was already on the last setting and to get it tighter I'd need a new chain. And, of course, when you get a new chain you also need new sprockets. Four days and $400 later, the new parts arrived, were fitted, and my bike was once again ready to ride. Unfortunately, I wasn't.

At this point you may be wondering what on earth possessed me to ride a motorbike around Australia, when I was so obviously afraid of it? Well, clearly, I didn't expect to be so scared (I wasn't like this at home). Before I left Glasgow, people had kept asking me, "Doesn't it scare you, the thought of riding around Australia by yourself?" I'd been far too excited to think about what could go wrong and I liked my own company so I wasn't bothered by this at all. But the reality of doing a big trip like this was proving to be very different from the dream.

I'd been on the road earlier than planned and, as a result, I hadn't had much time to get used to the new bike before having to ride it fully laden. The weather was harsh, the roads were different and I was riding like a complete novice. I'd spent most of the preceding fortnight scared out of my wits and I could feel the stress mounting in my body. I knew I needed to cry and let it all out, but I hadn't been able to find anywhere private enough to do so.

MONEY WORRIES

I was also starting to worry about the amount of money I was spending. I had been expecting to spend the first two months of my trip house-sitting, which meant my outgoings would be minimal. However, all this staying in hostels and extra expense on the bike was starting to add up. The global economic downturn meant the British pound was weak and the Australian dollar was strong, so I wasn't getting as many dollars for my pound as I'd done on previous trips. Additionally, the cost of living seemed to have increased significantly in Australia and fuel and food were a lot more expensive than I'd expected.

In a panic, I went back online to try and arrange another house-sit, as I knew if I kept spending at this rate my budget would never last me the year. I found a three-month house-sit in Mount Molloy in Northern Queensland, looking after a dog and a cat, so I applied. The only problem was that it was due to start on 9 January 2011 and, as the house-sit I was doing before it in Whyalla in South Australia would end on 1 January 2011, that would give me just nine days to cover almost 4,000 km to get there in time.

Once I realised this, I almost hoped that I wouldn't get it. But a few days later, I got a reply saying I had. While the thought of being in one place for three months was a great relief, the prospect of riding up to Queensland in the middle of what would, by then, be the peak of the Australian summer was quite daunting. The most I'd ridden in one day so far had only been 364.2 km and this journey would involve averaging about 450 km a day. I started seriously considering selling the bike and buying a car.

REACHING OUT

There was a notice in the lift at the YHA which suggested various acts of kindness one could do to help one's fellow travellers. So, to get myself out of my somewhat self-focussed, nervous state, I decided I would go and volunteer my services at the RSPCA office around the corner from the hostel.

I was only stuffing envelopes (hundreds of them), but they had an area through the back where they kept animals that had been handed in and, as it was kitten season, there had been lots of kittens coming in and out. One day I spent about half an hour stroking one mother and her litter of eight tiny black, grey and white kittens. At first, the mother was quite protective, pushing my hand away from the kittens with her paw, but after I'd stroked her for a while, she let me touch them. They were beautiful and it felt like a real honour.

Unfortunately, if they can't find homes for the kittens, they have to put them down. On hearing this, I immediately volunteered to take them all, but the lady in charge didn't seem to think that a motorcycle would make a suitable home for them.

After Lilly left, I got a new room-mate – a Swiss girl called Corrine. She was really fun, too. I'm not exactly sure what I did, but when she left she gave me a big hug and thanked me for really cheering her up.

The room felt very empty after she'd gone and I wished I'd taken Paula's number so I could have given her a call. A day or so later, though, a Malaysian lady arrived who thought I was "so cool" for riding a bike around Australia and I immediately liked her too.

It's very easy to meet people when you're travelling. Everyone is really friendly and outward-focussed, taking an interest in everything the world has to offer. When you're "settled", though, people tend to be much more inward-looking and more concerned with family issues and things that only affect them. Now I understand why I never really feel like I fit in when I'm "settled" – I connect better with people with an outward focus.

I also met some men during my stay at the YHA: a Dutch guy called Roland, an Aussie biker called Al and another Aussie guy named Bradley. One night, Bradley was too late for the shops, so I made him some pasta while Al regaled us with stories of working in the mines, close encounters with sharks and near-death experiences.

I liked Al – he was funny and entertaining – even though he was considerably shorter than me. And I think he liked me too as, when he was leaving, I bumped into him at the lifts and we had an awkward moment when he mumbled something about wishing me a good trip, went bright red and then rolled his eyes skywards as if to say, "Good one, mate, you totally messed that up!"

LIGHT'S VISION

The second week I was there, I decided to explore North Adelaide. What a beautiful part of the city it is – full of elegant old houses and open parklands. There is a lookout there called Light's Vision, which overlooks the whole city and the Adelaide Hills. I kept finding myself being drawn back there for hours at a time.

Despite all the lovely people I'd met, I was still feeling very vulnerable, so one day, up at Light's Vision, I let go and sobbed my heart out. I'd been so scared, so dejected and so disappointed with myself. I'd completely lost my confidence with the bike, I didn't really know why I'd come here or what I hoped to achieve, and the prospect of spending the next eleven months wandering aimlessly round this vast continent suddenly didn't seem as appealing anymore.

As I contemplated all my fear and dejection, I started meditating. And as I sat there, I began to realise that these feelings weren't limited to my failure to handle the bike well – it was all the pain of the previous few years coming out as well.

The closure of my massage clinic had hit me hard. Prior to opening it, I had bumped into a former colleague

I'd known twenty-five years previously, and we'd started dating. He now had his own very successful business and I was able to bounce all my ideas off him. He was tremendously supportive and encouraging and, before I knew it, I'd completely fallen for him.

But he was just out of a thirty-year marriage and was very insistent that he couldn't give me any kind of commitment. To me, a commitment meant something long-term like living together or marriage, so not having a commitment didn't bother me. It was only when I realised that he didn't even want to be my boyfriend that it really sank in what he was saying.

So I called it off. It broke my heart. He was the most gorgeous, intelligent, generous and inspiring person I'd met in years, but I knew that if he didn't want me, there was no point in hanging around.

I carried on with my plans and a few months later opened my doors for business. It was one of the scariest things I'd ever done. Most people say it's the most exciting part of having a business, but I actually cringed when the signage went up and I thought about all the expectations people would have. What if I couldn't help them? What if they thought I was rubbish? I should have realised then that this isn't the right attitude to have when one is about to embark on a business enterprise. But I was committed; I couldn't pull out now.

Self-belief is what one needs whenever one is about to start any new venture. I believed in my ability to open and run a business (I was fantastically well-organised), but I didn't believe in my ability to heal people. Oh, I was a great therapist, but I'd never seen myself as a healer and I certainly knew I wasn't a miracle worker – and a big part of me believed that that's what a lot of people would be looking for. I couldn't possibly meet that expectation.

After a short time, I also realised that, although I'd chosen the perfect building, it was in the wrong location and not enough people passed by to reap the kind of numbers I needed in order to reach my targets.

And so, a year later, I pulled the plug and closed it for the final time. I was inconsolable. The shame of such a public failure left me reeling.

In the previous eighteen months, I'd lost the man I adored, I'd lost my dream business and I'd lost all the profits from the sale of my flat. Everything I'd worked so hard for was gone. Worst of all, I had no idea what I should do next. I'd spent seven years and invested thousands of pounds in becoming the best therapist I could hope to be. I couldn't just walk away from that, could I? And what the hell would I do instead?

Thankfully, my dear friends Rolf and Felicity offered me a part-time job, running their office accounts. It saved me. It was only a couple of days a week but it gave me a sense of purpose and helped me feel good at something again.

I continued doing massage on a part-time basis and also took on another office-based part-time job, but I couldn't get over the overwhelming sense of failure which was clouding my every decision. I was afraid of making another wrong choice. What if I wasted more time and money on another career that would take me nowhere? I mean, let's face it, I wasn't getting any younger. And how was I ever going to meet a man if I didn't have any money to go out? I was afraid of everything – and I'd brought all that fear with me to Australia, where it was compounding the anxiety I'd been feeling on the motorbike. No wonder I was such a mess.

And as I sat there at Light's Vision, sobbing my heart out, I got my own vision. It was time to let go of this sense of failure, to move on and leave that all behind me. Besides, hadn't I come here to have fun and find love? From this point on, I knew that, even if I couldn't completely let go of my fears, I needed to find a way to enjoy myself, *despite* these fears.

As I realised this, I started feeling better. A flock of rainbow parakeets unexpectedly soared above me, as if to confirm I'd come to the right conclusion. Suddenly everything seemed brighter and I was full of gratitude at having the opportunity to do this trip.

MOVING ON

In spite of this revelation, a new chain and panniers and several rides around the city to try and overcome my nerves, I was still very jittery the night before I left Adelaide. So I did something I seldom do: I prayed.

"Ride with me," I pleaded. "Please ride with me." In my head I saw my old riding buddy Minna-Ella pull up beside me. Then I saw other riders I knew, and some famous bikers, like Ewan and Charley, ride alongside me, too. And I felt a little calmer.

I should mention at this point that I've never been a religious person. I don't like the idea of anyone telling you how to connect with God, but there's a part of me that likes to believe there is a God out there looking after us all, and when I'm scared, I seem to believe in Him more than I normally do.

So the next day, I saddled up and set off. It was hot and by the time I'd carried my stuff down to the ground floor and round to where I'd parked the bike, I was dripping with sweat. I'd repacked everything from my former bike-gear bag into the panniers, and transferred everything in the roll bag into the bike-gear bag. This reduced the height of my load and lowered my centre of gravity, but it didn't affect the overall weight of it. So I gingerly started to make my way out of the city.

At one point, a sign indicated that I should take a road to the right. It wasn't obvious which one, so I pulled into the right-hand lane, only to have a helpful car driver shout out to me that the way out of the city was the next right. Getting onto the correct road, I followed it up to a huge junction, beyond which it became a massive freeway. Concrete walls funnelled us up a long incline into the Adelaide Hills. Heavy freight was all around me.

"Bloody hell, look out," the voice in my head screamed, as a truck started pulling out ahead of me. I had hoped my little commune with God was going to mean I had a better ride today, but Judge Jill was more critical than ever. After an hour she was giving me such a hard time, I stopped in a parking area and gave her a right good talking to.

When I got back on the bike, something had changed and the fear had gone. I was actually *riding* the bike, rather than being a helpless passenger with no sense of control.

I wish I could say this lasted all day, but it was a particularly long and hot ride to my next stop, Ouyen, so it was difficult to sustain my new-found determination. But I arrived safely, with no major incidents, so I was happy with that.

I followed the SE Freeway from Adelaide to Murray Bridge and on to Tailem Bend, where I had a quick break.

From there, I joined the Mallee Highway, which passed through what was obviously flour country – miles and miles of wheat fields criss-crossed by railway tracks and flour silos at each station. It was good riding – long straights followed by gentle, sweeping bends across the railway lines.

It was beautiful, isolated country but the distances were enormous. It was 144 km to the next town, Lameroo. I couldn't do it all in one go, so I stopped in a lay-by and swallowed a bottle of water – the temperature was now in the high twenties. No other vehicles had passed me for a while, so I stepped out into the middle of the road and took some pictures of the endless expanse ahead and behind me.

The panniers were making a difference, but I was still nervous about stopping and starting. As I approached another town, where I thought I'd have a stop, the verges were all gravel.

Oh God. My heart sank. In an attempt to avoid the scree, I ended up parking about 100 m away from the shop I was aiming for. A short walk in the intense heat had me sweating in no time. Inside, I bought a bottle of water. I wandered out onto the verandah, where a mother and daughter, both wearing floral dresses and straw hats as if they'd just walked through a time warp from the 1950s, were sitting.

As I downed my water in one go, the mother turned to me and said, "Feeling the heat?"

"Just a bit," I replied.

"This is nothing, you know. It will get much hotter than this in the summer."

They told me they'd been there all of their lives and that they lived on one of the nearby farms, as did most of the people in the area. This accounted for why the towns were so few and far between, with such small populations (only about 200 people each). This didn't stop everyone from knowing everyone else, though, and, they assured me, it was quite a social community.

From Pinaroo to Ouyen it was another 137 km, with hardly a building in between. There wasn't much traffic on the roads so I was able to dawdle along at my own pace, but I had to keep stopping for water as the heat was drying me out. In one small township, which had a picnic area opposite the pub, I spent about twenty minutes paddling the bike back and forth, trying to find a space with a smooth enough surface to park on. As I said, my new-found confidence didn't last all day. I was all right as long as I was moving; it was just the stopping and starting that I still got nervous about.

My next destination was Lake Boga, where I'd do my first house-sit. It was only another day's ride from Ouyen and, as I had a day in hand, I spent two nights in Ouyen. There were no youth hostels on this route and I didn't have a tent so I had to check into a motel. It was the first time I'd had to do this and I flinched somewhat when I found out the nightly rate was three times as much as a night in a YHA. But it was great having a room to myself and I totally luxuriated in the space and privacy it provided.

Ouyen was a small town with a railway station, a hotel, two motels, a campsite and a few shops. It also had an outdoor swimming pool, but, much to my dismay, it wasn't due to open until the day after I planned to leave. By now the temperature had risen to about 28°C, so I was desperate to cool off. When I discovered there was also a swimming pool at the motel I was staying in (hidden behind a cane fence) and gleefully went to enquire how to get in, I was hugely disappointed to hear that the owner had recently sold the land off to someone else and that was why it had been cordoned off.

DROUGHT, FLOODS AND PLAGUES OF LOCUSTS

Leaving Ouyen, I continued east across the Mallee Highway to Piangil, another 94 km stretch, then joined the Murray Valley Highway south to Swan Hill. Here, there was a sudden change of scenery and I found myself in fruit country – vineyards and fruit farms as far as the eye could see. Australia had been suffering from a drought for the last ten years, but this winter the drought had finally broken and the country had been experiencing extensive flooding, a much-needed mercy for this area.

As I rode into Lake Boga, there was a sign saying, "Pull over if locusts impair your vision." At first, I thought I'd mis-read this, but my hosts later assured me there were indeed plagues of locusts everywhere. They even pointed out some hatchlings as we took the dogs for their first walk. Within the next month these would grow into huge swarms, capable of stripping whole fields, so the Council was doing what they could to kill them off early. I hoped I'd be long gone by the time they got to "stripping" size.

Later that day, the owners took me for a look around. Lake Boga was less a town and more a collection of houses scattered around the edge of the lake. It was an almost perfectly circular lake, with a road running most of the way round it. There was a small group of shops, beyond where the Murray Valley Highway formed a tangent with the lake, and a Yacht Club and the Catalina Flying Boat Museum on the lake's shore. The Catalinas were flying boats used in

World War II and a squadron of them had been based on the lake. The museum was built to commemorate this.

Lake Boga had obviously once been a popular holiday destination, as there were several motels nearby, but these were now in ruins as a result of the lake drying up. The lake had been connected to the irrigation system for the surrounding farmlands, so it now rarely held much water. During the drought it had completely dried up, creating a terrible stench in the area. Fortunately, the recent flooding had filled it for the first time in ten years, so I was getting to see it at its best. It was a beautiful setting.

The next day, the owners departed and left me in charge of two dogs and a cat. The dogs needed a lot of attention and I almost broke my toe as I fell down the stairs in the middle of my first night to let them out. The cat, though, only needed feeding and patting – that was enough for her.

DOGGIE DRAMAS

It turns out there is a lot more to house-sitting than meets the eye. I'd occasionally looked after my friend Lucy's dog before I left home, to get some practice in, but it seemed that merely taking a dog for a walk once a day was completely different from living with two of them.

One of the two dogs I was looking after was a big, long-haired, shaggy female (whom I'll call Shaggy) and the other was a small, short-haired, fuzzy male (I'll call him Fuzzy). Shaggy had recently got a barb stuck in her paw, which had been extracted by the vet, but the owners were worried it might go septic so they asked me to keep an eye on it.

The dogs had me up at the crack of dawn on my first day, demanding to be taken for a walk. We set off down a back road the owners had shown me. Although it was only just after 6 am, I could already feel the heat rising. The road was deserted but, anxious not to have them run off on my first day, I kept them both on the lead so that we could get used to each other. Shaggy was a headstrong, determined dog and when we got to a creek she decided she was going for a swim whether I liked it or not and almost pulled me in with her. As her owner had let her do this the previous day and she'd then come back on the lead without a fight, I relented and let her go in. After a quick splash around, much to my relief, she let me put her back on the lead too. After that, I thought I wasn't going to have any problems with them, but what did I know?

The next day, I let them both off the lead on the back road. I was a bit later getting going that morning and, by the time we got back to the main road, a couple of small kids were waiting for their school bus. Recognising them, Shaggy went charging off to say hello and bounced up at them. Although the kids didn't completely freak out, I could tell they didn't really like having a big hairy dog jump all over them, so after that I made sure I had Shaggy back on the lead long before we got anywhere near the main road.

After a few walks, I got bored going down the back road, so I decided to try going along the main road by the lakeside instead. This was really pretty, but involved going past a number of houses. As we got to a picnic area, another dog came charging out from a nearby house and barked ferociously at us. Shaggy and Fuzzy started barking and snarling back at it. Just as I thought the whole thing was going to descend into a wild dog fight, the owner came rushing out, put the other dog on its lead and shouted for me to "keep walking, keep walking". *Walk?* We practically ran out of there.

As there were only two walks I could take the dogs on, I couldn't really avoid taking them down the main road, so the next day I decided to try again. This time, I was ready for the wild hound and, just before we got to its house, we did a swift about-turn and headed back.

Feeling quite pleased with myself for masterminding this new strategy, I was immediately presented with another problem. A puppy in another house came running out to make friends. It was adorable, so I let it sniff and nuzzle my two dogs for a few minutes. However, we couldn't spend all day chatting and after a while I moved my dogs along.

Unfortunately, the puppy came too. In fact, no matter what I did, the puppy kept following us. I tried putting it back in its garden, I tried shooing it away, I tried knocking on the owners' door to see if they'd come and take it, I tried telling it to stay, but nothing worked. Eventually it followed us all the way home.

This wouldn't have been a problem, but "home" was about a 1.5 km walk away. Once I'd safely secured my dogs in their garden, I had to walk 1.5 km back to the puppy's house. As I was approaching, a ute[2] drew up with a rather puzzled-looking driver behind the wheel. This was the owner, so I explained what had happened, unleashed the little rascal and returned it. Then I had to walk another 1.5 km back to my house. In total, that "short" afternoon walk had ended up being about 6 km long for me.

Not to be put off by such inconveniences, I took the dogs back down the road the next day, too. It was very hot and Shaggy wanted a swim, so I let her off the lead and she plunged into the lake. I could see the joy in her eyes and when I called for her to come out she was having none of it. This was the best fun she'd had in ages and going home for dinner just didn't compare.

She ended up staying in that lake for about half an hour and there was nothing I could do to get her out again. Eventually I had to wade into the shallows and collar her when she swam by. Then, just as I thought my troubles were over, the mad puppy came bounding out again as we passed his house on our way back. Fortunately the owner was in this time, so I was able to get him to retrieve it.

Fuzzy was a much easier dog to handle. He was dainty and wanted to please. In fact, he seemed as annoyed with Shaggy's antics as I was getting. All he wanted to do was snuggle up on the couch and be petted.

By the next day, Shaggy's paw was looking rather red and pus-filled, so I decided to take her to the vet's. As the vet was in Swan Hill, about 20 km away, and I obviously couldn't take her on the bike, I enlisted the help of some neighbours, who very kindly brought their four-wheel drive around and put her in the back. The vet advised that they'd need to do an X-ray to see if there was anything still stuck in the dog's paw and, if so, they'd need to operate and keep her in overnight.

It turned out that a shard of wood had actually got stuck between Shaggy's toes, so when we picked her up the next day, she'd got a bandage around her foot, a cone on her head to stop her scratching it, and had also been diagnosed with infections in each ear. She had been prescribed antibiotics for the foot and drops for the ears and I was instructed not to let her into any water until the ear drops were finished and the foot had healed.

This was not going to be easy. Shaggy loved her swimming and, as the temperature was now about 30°C, she was not going to thank me for depriving her of her daily dip.

The next day, I decided to stick to the back road and take a different branch that looked as if it would avoid the creek. Fortunately, it did, and I felt quite chuffed with myself for finding it. What I forgot was that Shaggy had a small plastic pool in the back garden – and when we got home the first thing she did was clamber in and have a soak. The vet had given me strict instructions not to let her bandage get wet or it would have to come off. So, less than twenty-four hours after collecting her, I'd failed in my duties already.

To avoid that happening again, I emptied the pool out and kept to the new route for the next day or so. But, at the end of one walk, Shaggy decided it was swim time whether I wanted her to go in or not, and dragged me down to the lakeside. I managed to bring her to a stop on the road just before the water's edge and we ended up having a half-hour Mexican standoff, where she sat in the road refusing to move and I tried to coax her back. Eventually my patience (or should I say stubbornness?) won out and she reluctantly followed me home.

My first few attempts at putting her ear drops in were reasonably successful in that I managed to get them in, but not without making Shaggy feel very uncomfortable. When I tried the third lot, she rolled her head away and started snarling at me. As her owners were due back the next day, I decided to leave it to them.

Despite all this and being swarmed by locusts, dragonflies and other airborne insects, having to walk in temperatures of about 30°C, picking barbs out of the dogs' paws, having them follow me about for pretty much twenty-four hours a day, looking after the cat, the general housekeeping and all the gardening duties, I had a brilliant week in Lake Boga. The animals were so loving and all the walking improved my fitness and reduced my waistline considerably. Plus I met some lovely people – like the neighbour who gave me a lift back from the Post Office the day I decided to walk down to the shops, not realising it was a 7 km walk each way.

FLASHING LIGHTS

I left Lake Boga on Monday 1 November 2010 and rode the 366.4 km back to Melbourne. It was a sunny day but quite chilly; nevertheless, I made good progress.

Somewhere between Echuca and Bendigo, a big orange light started flashing on my dashboard. Thinking this was the oil light, I pulled over and poured in half a bottle of oil. However, on restarting, the light didn't go out. As I was getting low on petrol and needed to find a garage anyway, I decided to press on regardless, all the time thinking, Funny, why would the oil light stay on when I've just added more oil?

Then it struck me: this wasn't the oil light at all. It was the fuel light, telling me I'd gone onto the reserve tank. *Doh!* Luckily I managed to make it to a petrol station before running out, so all was well.

The panniers were now making a big difference to the handling of the bike and I felt my old confidence starting to return as I neared Melbourne. I even found myself whooping out loud as the city skyline came into view.

So, five and a half weeks after leaving, I was back in Melbourne, having completed what seemed like a trial run. In effect, I'd done a small circuit from Melbourne to Adelaide to Lake Boga and back to Melbourne again.

It gave me a taste of some of the challenges of riding a motorbike in such a massive country and showed me how vulnerable I could be.

Now I just needed to decide whether I wanted to continue to put myself at risk by doing a major circuit of the country or not.

Chapter 8: Decision Time

CREATURE COMFORTS

The next month in Melbourne was lovely. Apart from a few torrential downpours, the weather warmed up and I was able to get out and about and explore the local, and not so local, area. And, of course, I got to walk my friends' two gorgeous whippets every day. One of them, Oscar, loved chasing things, so one day I picked up a ball and carried it down to the park in my hand. He kept jumping up and lightly nudging my hand as we walked, as if to say, "Throw the ball, please throw the ball." It was one of those moments of pure, simple joy.

They were such delightful creatures – so friendly and obedient and affectionate. On a couple of the cooler nights they even burrowed under my covers and spent the night keeping me cosy. And the unexpected bonus was that I lost about half a stone in weight and got a lot fitter.

DECISIONS, DECISIONS ...

When I returned to Melbourne, I was in a bit of a quandary about whether I should sell the bike and get a car. Because I would be there for a month, there would be enough time to sell it, but surprisingly I found I was quite reluctant to do so.

When I told Lisa and Lou that I'd got a house-sit in Mount Molloy and that I only had nine days to ride the

4,000 km to get there, Lou immediately tried to dissuade me. According to him, the distances were too vast, the heat too intense and, given my inexperience and somewhat shaky start, this was an unwise choice for me.

Lisa then piped in, "You know, I would usually encourage you to do whatever you want to do, but in this case, I have to say I'm with Lou."

With such sceptical feedback, I felt perhaps they had a point. So I looked into all the options which would avoid the 4,000 km ride to Queensland. These included buying or renting a car; putting the bike on motorail from Adelaide to Darwin (but I'd still need to ride it to Adelaide and then from Darwin to Queensland); riding it halfway and leaving it somewhere like Brisbane, then flying to Whyalla and back to Brisbane then picking up the bike and continuing northwards. But none of them were going to be easy or cheap.

And besides, I was discovering that the ridiculous amount of luggage I was carrying was having one very positive side-effect – it was helping me to connect with people. Before I left the UK, I'd lost a lot of my social confidence and had started to think people weren't interested in anything I had to say. But the fear of dropping the bike under its massive load, strangely enough, brought me out of my shell. It gave me something to talk about and I happily told everyone I met about the problems it was giving me.

Much to my surprise and delight, they seemed to like hearing about it and were interested in lots of other things I had to say too. Without my excess baggage, I'm not sure so many people would have commented on it and that there would have been so many opportunities to speak to people as a result. It started to rebuild my faith in myself as a person people would like. Maybe this was something I needed to do?

One day, I decided to see what I'd get for the bike if I sold it. I took it back to the place I'd bought it from, but it turned out they weren't buying any new stock and, even if they had been, I'd have only got about half of what I'd paid for it. So this put an end to my swithering and I decided to keep it.

Funnily enough, I found myself enormously relieved by this decision. I guess I wasn't ready to give up the adventure just yet, after all.

NEXT STOP

Whilst in Melbourne, I also had to decide where to go next. One of Lisa's friends, a guy called Nick who lived in Canberra, had contacted me while I was still in the UK to see if I'd like a riding buddy for any of the trip. I hadn't been very keen on the idea at first as I knew I wasn't a fast rider and I didn't want to put pressure on myself by having to keep up with someone else. However, by this stage I was beginning to think it might be quite nice to have some company for a while. So, as I had three and a half weeks before I needed to be in Whyalla, I decided to go to Tasmania for two weeks (the weather was warmer now and, as the ferry leaves from Melbourne, it seemed like the perfect opportunity to make the trip). I would then meet up with Nick in Canberra, from where we'd ride across to Adelaide together. After that, he would make his way back to Canberra and I'd continue on to Whyalla.

I also decided to abandon my OU courses. Even though I had almost a month in Melbourne, I couldn't get myself to do any studying, so after two weeks of beating myself up about it I admitted defeat and sent my books home.

This meant there was now much more room in my former bike-gear bag. So I went out and bought a tent, a collapsible stool, a self-inflating sleeping mat, a camping stove and a hydration pack to carry water in, to add to the sleeping bag that was already in there. Having just managed to lighten my load slightly, the addition of more camping equipment meant I'd actually added even more weight to my pack. Had I learnt nothing about the perils of riding with too much luggage?

Chapter 9: Tasmanian Turning Point

SPIRIT OF TASMANIA

I booked my ticket to Tasmania for Friday 26 November 2010. I was certain that the ferry, the *Spirit of Tasmania*, was at 5.30 pm and that check-in, being two and a half hours before, was at 3.00 pm, so Lou guided me down to the ferry terminal for precisely that time.

It was my first time back on the bike in a month and I was nervous again. Hopping my leg over, I was relieved to find that the additional weight of the camping gear didn't make the bike any more difficult to handle. We set off down the Tullamarine Freeway for the city. Within a few minutes, the dark storm clouds that had been gathering all day let go of their charge and soon I was struggling to see what was ahead.

If you've ever wondered how motorcyclists keep their visors clear when it's pouring with rain and they have no windscreen wipers – the answer is, with great difficulty. You're supposed to use a finger to wipe the raindrops off, but when you're on a busy freeway, trying to follow the car ahead, with vehicles cutting past you in all directions, the last thing you want to do is take your hand off the handlebars.

Coming into the downtown area, we joined a huge tailback of traffic merging to get past some roadworks. Three lanes were trying to form one, and Lou suddenly got separated from me. I filtered to the left, but when I emerged from the other side of the obstruction the rain was obscuring my vision and I couldn't see him anywhere.

Shit, what am I going to do, I panicked. I had no idea how to get to the ferry terminal without him. Then, as I pulled out to pass the car ahead of me, I saw him sitting in front of it. I'd been looking too far ahead and had missed him. Pulling back in behind him, I sat on Lou's tail for the rest of the journey.

Going over the Bolte Bridge, the skies cleared, giving fantastic views of the Yarra River and the city below. Shortly after, we took an exit and descended into a web of roundabouts and housing estates, before popping out at the ferry terminal. Heaven knows how I would have found it without Lou.

On arrival, the man at the gate advised me that boarding would commence at 4.30 pm, not 3 pm as I'd expected. I thought this was a bit odd, but didn't question it. However, when at 5.30 pm we were all still waiting to board and I was informed that boarding wouldn't commence until 6.00 pm, I fished out my ticket, only to discover that the ferry was actually scheduled to leave at 7.30 pm, not 5.30 pm. I'd converted 19.30 on the 24-hour clock to 5.30 on the normal one.

The extra wait was not wasted, though. I met a big group of bikers from Western Australia (WA), and another couple of guys from WA called Pat and Martin, who kept me amused. There was also a group of bikers from the Australian Outlaws, but they were a bit too scary so I didn't talk to them.

When, at six o'clock, the gates opened and boarding commenced, I was directed round the front of the ship into what seemed to be a car park. I was now going in the opposite direction to the ferry, and, confused, I stopped and mouthed to the people in the car behind me, "Where do I go?"

It was only when they pointed to the left that I noticed a long, steep, narrow ramp rising into the heavens like the Golden Gate Bridge, delivering vehicles into the belly of the ship.

Jesus Christ, I thought as I stared, horrified, at the slope. It was a metal ramp with a smooth, shiny surface – all it needed was another shower of rain and it would be like a skating-rink. But I couldn't dilly dally – even the nice people in the car behind were getting impatient – so I just had to ride on up.

"Keep your eye on where you want to go," I kept telling myself. "The bike will only go where you point it."

It was tempting to look out to the sides, but I knew that with one wrong move I could end up over the edge or sliding all the way back down again. As I slithered to a halt at the top, I was directed to a section in the middle where some deckhands were waiting to strap down the bike. Dismounting, I noticed that Pat and Martin were next to me, so I vented my horror about the perilous ascent, unstrapped my bag and made my way up to my cabin. Having learnt from my European ferry rides, I'd had the foresight to pack my small backpack with overnight gear, so I was able to leave the rest of my load on the bike.

It was an overnight crossing from Melbourne to Devonport, so the following morning I rolled off the ferry, down a much gentler ramp, to start my loop of Tassie. Devonport was right in the middle of the northern coast, giving me a choice of whether I went east or west when I disembarked. So far, my route had pretty much been dictated by where the next youth hostel was located, and Tassie was to be no different. I headed east.

I followed the highway out of Devonport and then took a back road to Port Sorrel, a pleasant little town on a big sandy sea inlet. After that, I rode through acres of rolling farmlands to Exeter, where I stopped for breakfast and a visit to the Tourist Information office to buy a National Parks pass.

Turning left out of Exeter took me along the side of the Tamar River to the Batman Bridge (named after one of the first British settlers in the southern antipodes, not the Caped Crusader of Gotham City fame). Crossing the bridge, I continued north to George Town, a somewhat bigger town, towards the northern end of the Tamar River.

A short wander round and I was back on the bike, doing the final cross-country section to Bridport, where I checked into the YHA. There was a group of gardening enthusiasts there who were on a tour of private gardens in the area. They were very friendly and one lady, Anne, took great interest in my trip and even gave me her number to contact when I got to Hobart, which I thought was incredibly nice, not to mention trusting.

A very intense young man called James also checked in and did his best to convince me he was totally over his ex-girlfriend – by talking about her all night.

The warden was very friendly and, as there was a band on at the local hotel, he, James and I arranged to go and see it. Unfortunately the whole town experienced a blackout that night when a car ran into a power line, so we had to abandon that outing.

WATER

The next day, I set off for St Helens. The ride started really well, passing through lots of lilac poppy fields (which I later discovered were opium poppies, grown strictly for medicinal purposes, people assured me) and gentle rolling hills topped with wispy clouds. As I left a small town called Derby, the rain started, and as the road wound its way up into the cloud base I found myself in a torrential downpour.

The road continued to climb and quickly developed into 25 km of continuous hairpin bends, which passed through the most beautiful rainforest, thick with dark green foliage, huge green ferns and tall trees draped in vines. I zigzagged my way along, hardly daring to take my eyes off the road ahead, and the rain kept pouring.

Down into second to take a bend, back up into third for a small straight, then down into second again for another bend. The verge fell away to my left, leaving a huge open gully below.

"Jesus," I gasped, as I dropped into first just to be safe. Then back up to second, then first again as another bend clung to the exposed hillside.

My visor kept fogging up and I had to partially open it to keep it clear. Even though it was only cracked open by half an inch or so, it was enough to let the water in, which pricked my eyes, making it even harder to see what was in front of me. My mirrors had also fogged up and it was equally tricky to see what was behind.

Interestingly, although it was difficult riding, I found I was quite enjoying it. There were hardly any other vehicles on the road and I was able to get into a bit of a rhythm, winding my way through the bends without the pressure of any traffic behind me.

At the end of the pass was a long clearing with nothing in it but a small roadhouse. I was completely drenched by this time, so I decided to stop and warm up. My boots were full of water and squelched loudly as I made my way across the forecourt into the café. After a warming cup of tea and an all-day breakfast, I stepped back outside to discover that the rain had stopped. Relieved, I filled up the tank and continued on to St Helens.

The hostel I had hoped to stay in wasn't going to open for three hours. As I was still soaked and starting to feel quite shivery, I decided to book into a nearby holiday cabin instead, which had a bath available. It was utter bliss, sinking into the pool of hot water. As I lay there soaking up the heat, it struck me how strange it is that water can blind you or heal you, depending on the circumstances.

BAY OF FIRES

I awoke the next morning to clear blue skies and sunshine, so I packed up the bike and rode the half-mile down the road to the backpackers' hostel and checked in there. I unloaded the bike and took the road to Billabong Bay to see the Bay of Fires. This is actually a series of bays with white sandy beaches and turquoise waters. It is so named because the beaches are flanked by large boulders covered in a sort of brown algae, which looks fiery red when the sun shines.

It was a beautiful ride, with wide, open views out across the bays to the ocean beyond. Unburdened by my usual heavy load, I found I was soaring along, wind in my hair, free as a bird. It was a narrow and bendy road, but today it didn't seem to matter. I was cruising along.

Another road took me round to the other side of the bay, where there were more fabulous white beaches. At the end of the road, there was a boat ramp and a small jetty that stretched into the sea. The water was so clear and the sun so bright I was on the verge of stripping off and going in for a swim, when a van full of Park Rangers drove up and started unloading a marine observation vessel. I thought better of it and decided to take a walk round the headland to another beach instead. It only took thirty minutes, but seeing as I was still in full motorcycle apparel, I was soaked in sweat by the time I got back to the bike.

That night, I met a French lady in the hostel. Her English was a bit patchy so I endeavoured to fill in the missing words with my schoolgirl French. We ended up having quite a good conversation and I felt quite pleased with myself for managing to string a few sentences together.

HUMAN KINDNESS

The next morning, I said au revoir to my new French friend and headed south for Coles Bay and the Freycinet National Park, which houses Wineglass Bay, one of Tasmania's top tourist attractions. The hostel manager Paul, a keen biker, suggested I should take the road to St Mary's instead of going all the way along the coast.

This took me up the St Mary's Pass and down the Elephant Pass – both narrow, twisty roads but, compared to my rainforest epic the day before, a piece of cake. On my way down I even passed some of the WA boys, who were on their way up.

I passed some more of them outside the Motorcycle Museum at Bicheno, but as I didn't know it was there until

I was level with it, and pulling up would have involved executing something of an emergency stop, a manoeuvre I didn't yet feel confident enough to pull off without landing in a rather undignified heap at their feet, I just sailed on by.

My riding skills were improving, but stopping and starting were still testing me every time. Plus, I was starting to recognise that I had another problem apart from the weight of the bike – I don't have very good balance. I'd had a bad back injury in 1996 and although it didn't really stop me doing most things, it meant I sat slightly lopsided on the bike, as Minna-Ella and one of my instructors had observed. Apart from looking odd, I hadn't thought too much about it, but could it be that this is what made it so difficult for me to handle my load? Was the weight exacerbating an otherwise innocuous problem?

I got to Coles Bay about 1 pm, checked into what can best be described as a "traditional" YHA (i.e. needing a lot of work) and headed off in search of the Freycinet National Park. By a remarkable stroke of good luck (rather than navigation), I quickly found myself at the start of the Wineglass Bay walk.

Having strapped my jacket to the bike, I set off, this time just in my bike trousers, boots and a T-shirt. After a short distance the path splits and you have the option of going directly to the Bay itself (three hours) or going to a viewpoint instead (one and a half hours). Always looking for the easy option, I decided to take the viewpoint route. I should have realised that it would be higher than the beach and that the path would go up a hill – but this path turned out to be nearly vertical. Not being a particularly keen hill walker and being somewhat weighed down in my heavy gear, it took me almost two hours to do the one and a half hour walk. But it was worth it in the end, as the view of the bay was fabulous.

Wineglass Bay, as its name suggests, forms a perfect wineglass shape encircled by a long, white, sandy beach. If it hadn't been so overcast, I'm sure the waters would have been as clear and blue as they were in the Bay of Fires, but the lack of sunshine meant the colours weren't quite as radiant as they had been the day before.

That night I decided to have a break from my usual diet of pasta and to eat in the local pub. I was directed into a waiting area and, shortly afterwards, a couple about the same age as me were ushered in. Nodding acknowledgements to each other, we soon got talking. Wendy and Ross had come across from northern Victoria with a caravan to spend their honeymoon touring around Tassie. They invited me to join them for dinner and, as they were into dirt biking, we had a long conversation about bikes and the adventures we'd had.

They were warm, generous people and when I told them how shabby the hostel was, they invited me to pitch my tent in their camping space. It was a lovely offer but in the end I decided to tough it out in the hostel, seeing as I'd already paid for my bed.

Meeting them really brightened up my evening and, at the end, they even paid for my meal. I was really touched by their friendship and generosity.

Next morning I went to the bakery for breakfast and got talking to some people who were part of a group of bikers over from Sydney. When I finished eating, I paid for my food, put my wallet in my jacket and returned to the hostel.

As I came back out a few minutes later, one of the bikers was leaving a note on my bike, saying he'd found my wallet and had put it in my backpack. Unbeknown to me, it had fallen through the gap between the pocket and the lining of my jacket onto the bakery floor.

God, imagine if he hadn't found it and I'd gone riding off without it? I could have gone for miles before I noticed and I wouldn't have had a clue where I'd lost it. So, again, I was humbled by the kindness of strangers.

LOSS OF CONCENTRATION

Leaving Coles Bay, I rejoined the main road south. This weaves its way along the coastline to Triabunna, where I decided to turn into the town for a look around. As I was approaching a junction I somehow managed to put the bike in neutral (instead of first) and ended up going into the turn without power. I managed to get my foot down in time to stop the bike keeling over, but it made me realise I was starting to lose my concentration so I had an extended lunch break there.

The roads were much better in Tassie than on the mainland. Despite being quite twisty, they didn't have the same extreme camber and gravel verges that I'd had to deal with in Victoria and South Australia. They actually reminded me a lot of the roads in Scotland and I felt much more comfortable riding them.

I've always preferred riding on small back roads, eschewing the faster highways wherever possible in favour of the slower, more scenic routes. Apart from anything else, they were generally a lot quieter and I didn't feel so intimidated by the other traffic. Even though I was travelling along the main road around Tasmania, the volume of traffic was minimal and I felt a lot more relaxed.

After lunch, I continued along the Tasman Highway to Orford, where it heads inland along the side of a river. It was a beautiful stretch of road, with the river babbling along on one side and pine forests on the other. I continued to Sorrel, where I had another stop.

There happened to be a library right next to the spot I'd parked in, so I went inside and grabbed an internet terminal to check my email. While I was sitting there in my full riding gear, with my hair matted to my head, a man came in and sat opposite me. He kept smiling at me, which, feeling I looked somewhat less than my best, puzzled me greatly. My love life had been a patchy affair for the last twenty-five years. I'd had quite a few boyfriends after leaving school and through my early twenties, but from my first trip to Australia onwards, I went through several six-year periods of being alone, then going out with someone for a few years, then being alone again. I was currently on another long, dry spell and, given everything that had happened in the last few years, my confidence was pretty low. I knew I wasn't unattractive, but I certainly didn't feel like a stunner either. Surely this guy didn't think I looked good?

Reconnected with the world and feeling somewhat buoyed by this unexpected bit of interest, I tried to decide if I should continue south to Port Arthur or head west to Hobart. Wendy and Ross had recommended going to Port Arthur, as it had a large convict museum which was supposed to be very interesting and a beautiful viewpoint on the way, but it was another 80-odd km drive and I was starting to get tired. Hobart, on the other hand, was only 35 km away. It was now mid-afternoon so, after a while, I decided Hobart was the better option.

I entered Hobart from the east on the Tasman Highway, which becomes the Tasman Bridge spanning the Derwent

River. It was a spectacular crossing, enhanced by the fact that the sun had now come out.

I felt particularly pleased with myself for finding the street where the YHA was located on my first attempt. I had to do a few circuits of the one-way system, though, to position myself far enough down the street to ride the bike to the door.

When I checked in, the warden suggested I could leave the bike in a lane down the side of the hostel. Instantly forgetting my previous experiences of wardens trying to be helpful, I unloaded all my gear into the foyer and attempted to do this. Unfortunately, it was quite a narrow lane with a downwards slope and to get the bike over the kerb I had to power it in nose first, which meant I wouldn't then be able to get it back out again. I tried to manoeuvre it so it was pointing outwards but there wasn't enough room to turn it around. So eventually I had to get off and push it back onto the pavement and out onto the street. I tried again to reverse it in but just didn't have the strength to get it over the kerb without engine power, so I abandoned the idea and rode it over to a dedicated motorcycle parking bay, a street away, instead.

By the end of all this, and carrying my gear up six flights of stairs to the third floor (there was no lift at this hostel), I was once again sweating like a pig – this was becoming an unpleasant side effect of travelling with too much luggage.

Given that it took me about one and a half hours to park and unload, I was glad I'd decided to skip Port Arthur and come straight to Hobart.

CONVICT ROOTS

To get a better understanding of the lie of the land in Hobart, I joined the Hop On Hop Off bus the next day. The driver was really excellent and gave a very informative commentary of the history and geography of the area.

Hobart lies in a bay on the southern coast of the island. After Sydney, it was the second place in Australia to be colonised by the British, who originally thought it was part of the mainland.

The first settlers barely survived, as the seeds they had brought with them from home rotted during the long voyage, leaving them with no way of cultivating food. Fortunately for them, a second wave of settlers arrived just in time with a healthier seed stock. Land was fertile, so the settlers fenced off large sections of it to make farms, displacing the local Aboriginal population in the process. Battles ensued as the Aboriginals lost more of their traditional hunting grounds.

In 1828, the fighting was so bad that martial law was declared and the Aboriginals were forced at gunpoint from districts settled by the whites. Between 1829 and 1834, all remaining Aborigines were resettlcd to Flindlers Island, off the north coast of Tasmania, where, within 32 years, they all perished (another shameful event in our bloody history). As further waves of settlers and convicts arrived, they learnt how to master the land, and Hobart soon became a prospering city.

Today, Hobart is a busy little sea port. A pretty marina merges with the central business area, which climbs its way up the lower slopes of the surrounding hillsides. A series of long streets run from north to south and are criss-crossed by a matrix of smaller streets going east to west. The road that runs around the harbour area extends east and west along the coast to busy suburbs.

One of the stops on the tour was the Female Factory, which was the old female prison in the days of transportation[3]. After serving their time in the Female Factory for various crimes and misdemeanours, the women would be assigned to work for free settlers, many of whom were men who had left their families at home. Needless to say, the "assignees", either willingly or unwillingly, became the objects of the settlers' affections and usually ended up pregnant – a "crime" for which they were sent back to the Female Factory.

Most of the babies were born there, too, but few survived and something like 12,000 were buried on the site of the old prison. Strangely enough, many of the assignees deliberately got pregnant, as life in the Female Factory was actually better than it was in service. Many of them were raped or attacked while out of prison, so, in some ways, being locked up was safer than being free. I'm not usually too concerned with women's issues, but I found this a really shocking story.

In fact, I found the whole subject of transportation really fascinating. People would be sent out to the Colonies for the duration of their sentences and then, when they were released, they pretty much had to settle where they'd been sent, as few of them had the funds to buy their passage home. Apparently, this is where the term "life sentence" comes from – if you were sent to the Colonies, you'd be there for life.

Interestingly, many of the released prisoners went on to become quite successful. Land was plentiful and after all the Aboriginals had been annihilated by the British army it was relatively easy for people to settle and build lives for themselves.

TASMANIAN HOSPITALITY

The next day, I met up with my gardening enthusiast friend, Anne, from the Bridport YHA. As I'd only met her once, I was a bit worried I wouldn't recognise her. Standing outside the hostel waiting for her, I found myself jumping every time a car went by with someone who looked even remotely like her. Anne was a tallish lady in her late fifties, with short, white hair. I had no need to be concerned, though, as I knew her immediately.

She greeted me with a warm smile and treated me to tea in a café near the Female Factory. She was open and easy to talk to and I was really glad I'd made the effort to look her up. I told her about my experience at the Female Factory and she explained that, until recently, most Tasmanians weren't interested in their convict roots – in fact, most of them were deeply ashamed of them. In the last few years, though, there had been an upsurge of interest, which had resulted in many of the old jails being opened to the public and information on the convicts becoming more freely available.

Afterwards, Anne took me for a tour of the local beaches near her home. Hobart stretches out east and west into suburbs which flank the shores of the bay, creating some fabulous views. In the evening, she took me back to her house to meet her family and have a barbeque. One of her sons, Richard, a good-looking guy in his late twenties, had temporarily moved back home. He was quite shy, but once I discovered he was into *drifting*, something I'd never heard of before, and bombarded him with questions about it, he opened right up and we got on really well.

Drifting is a motorsport in which drivers deliberately over-steer their cars, causing a loss of traction of the rear wheels, while they try and maintain control from entry to exit of a corner – that's skidding their way round the corners to you and me. As well as being a mechanic, Richard was also a driver for one of the local teams and obviously loved it.

They were fun, caring people and, sitting round their dinner table sharing such wonderful food and company, I felt a touch of sadness as I knew I'd soon have to leave and be on my own again. Although I loved the sociability of hostels, being in the warmth of a real home was a genuine delight and it was lovely to spend time with Anne and be looked after for a day. I was deeply grateful.

I left Hobart on the Saturday and headed south to a small village called Dover. It was a long and twisty ride along the coast and by the time I got to a place called Cygnet, I was exhausted. However, that was only half way. From Cygnet, the road went inland for a while until it met the Huon River, which it crossed at Huonville. From there I picked up the Huon Highway and continued south along the banks of the river. It was very pretty riding, with tree-covered hills on one side and lots of boats on the river. Several boat clubs were located on its banks and there seemed to be a regatta going on.

On arriving at Dover, I booked into the local caravan park and, for the first time, pitched my tent. It was surprisingly roomy inside for a one-man job, so I was pleased with my choice. I went to the supermarket, only to discover there was a backpackers' hostel right behind it. I didn't wimp out, though, and after cooking some dinner on my camping stove spent quite a comfortable night in my little orange home.

It turned out there wasn't much to see at Dover – it was just a pretty little bay – so I decided not to linger there. The next day was a massive ride. I rode all the way from Dover in the far south to Queenstown in the far west, a distance of some 400-odd km. I didn't exactly set out to do this: it was just the way things worked out. First I had to ride back to Hobart, then take the road north-west out of the city. I was surprised at how far north the city extended beyond the central business area, and I had to deal with a long series of traffic lights to clear the city limits.

Once clear, though, the traffic thinned and the road started to follow the Derwent River inland. The next 200 km were quite pastoral, climbing up and down long, undulating hillsides. Initially, I had thought I would go as far as Tarraleah, where I'd be able to camp for the night, but when I got there the campground was located at the end of a long gravel track so I decided to keep going. Although I was feeling more comfortable on Tasmanian roads, I still didn't feel ready to tackle a dirt road.

Next, I thought about trying the campsite at Bronte's Park, as I had to go there for petrol anyway. The petrol station was situated on a rough and rocky forecourt, which I had to paddle my way in and out of, and when I saw that the campground was accessed from a similar surface, I quickly decided against it too.

The campground at Derwent Bridge had the same problem. It looked as if the National Park camping area at Lake St Claire would be a good bet, as the road to the lake was sealed, but then I discovered I had no cash left and wouldn't be able to pay for it so, once again, I had to keep going.

I was quite disappointed about missing that campsite, as it looked as if it would have been a beautiful spot. Half the problem was that it was a very overcast day and I was feeling a bit miserable, so I was finding it difficult to get enthusiastic about anything. However, after I passed Lake St Clair, the sun came out and my whole mood lifted.

The final 86 km from there to Queenstown were through the Franklin-Gordon Wild Rivers National Park, which was absolutely beautiful. The road rose up into the mountains, which afforded spectacular views of scrubland and jagged mountain tops, and then descended through valleys draped with rainforest.

The final section took me back uphill and round the southern end of Lake Burbury, which was surrounded by imposing dark peaks. From there, the road wove up through barren, red rock faces which had once housed a thriving copper mining industry. Riding up through these led to a summit, from which I could see what appeared to be a still-functioning mine. I then had a very steep and twisty descent into Queenstown through more scarred rock faces.

Having left Dover at 10 am, I arrived at Queenstown at 6 pm. Once again, I couldn't find a suitable campground, so I determined to press on to Strahan, another 40 km ride, even though I was weak with exhaustion. Fortunately, on the way out of the town I saw a motel offering "backpackers-style accommodation". It wasn't the nicest place I've stayed in, but I was so tired I didn't care.

Queenstown had obviously fallen on hard times. As I wandered around, trying to find a place to eat, I saw arcades of shop units that were closed down, hotel facades that were crumbling and windows that were boarded up.

A handful of people were leaving the supermarket as it shut for the night. I spotted a pizza place that was still open so I ordered one. They were clearly on the ball, as they had a couple of internet terminals set up which patrons could use for free and non-patrons for a charge.

Despite its somewhat dilapidated appearance, I liked Queenstown. It was surrounded by high cliffs on one side and pine forests on the other and had a nostalgic feel about it. I could imagine times gone by, with mine workers staggering out of bars into crowded streets, the air filled with the sound of piano music, raucous laughter and drunken arguments. I felt sure that, once the summer season got underway in earnest, it would spring back to life again.

After a good night's sleep I left Queenstown early the following morning and rode the last stretch to Strahan. More steep, twisty roads lay ahead, but thankfully all the traffic was going in the opposite direction so I had a clear run.

When I arrived in Strahan, I parked the bike and wandered over to the wharf. There was a guy offering motorcycle tours – Al's Motorcycle Tours – so I started chatting to him. He was a big man in his fifties, with a shaven head and the usual leather waist-jacket and jeans. He offered to take me for a ride around the town on the back of his Harley, so I happily accepted.

God, this guy really knew how to handle a big motorcycle. He had me up and down hills, whizzing round bends and doing U-turns in areas the size of a postage stamp. Afterwards he asked me if I'd like to have tea (dinner) with him that evening, so I said yes. He then cooked me the mother of all barbeques. There was steak, pork chops, lamb chops, sausages, onions – you name it.

It was a glorious feast and between us we managed to consume the whole lot. In my zeal I spilled relish down the front of my white T-shirt and, in an attempt to wash it off, ended up soaking the front of it, which rendered it transparent.

Needless to say, Al didn't seem to mind this at all. I wasn't quite sure what his intentions were and kept thinking, There's no such thing as a free lunch, you know. But Al turned out to be a perfect gentleman and took me back to the hostel, with only a short detour to a local viewpoint to watch the sun go down.

HARD LABOUR

Strahan sits on a large sea inlet called McQuarrie Harbour, so the next day I took a boat tour of this and the Gordon River, which flows into it. It's a massive bay and it took a good hour just to get to the confluence with the ocean. The boat then headed back into the bay, where we stopped to see an island that had once housed some of Tasmania's most hardened criminals.

Only the roughest men and women were sent there, and our guide showed us how they lived. The settlement was a ruin now, but you could still see the remains of the boatyards where they worked and the buildings where they ate and slept. It was like a small village, with a bakery, tannery, church and other small structures.

Several of the convicts tried to escape, but it was miles to land so only one or two of them made it to freedom. Most were picked up by floating patrols and returned, only to have their sentences lengthened.

From here, the boat made its way inland up the Gordon River. The ship's captain gave an interesting commentary about the former logging industry which had once thrived in the region. This part of Tasmania was famous for the Huon Pine, a type of wood favoured by the boat-building industry. Teams of men would row small boats with enough supplies for two or three months from Strahan up the Gordon River, and then walk into the forest and make camp. They'd selectively fell as many Huon Pines as they could before their supplies ran out. The logs would be floated back down the river to McQuarrie Harbour, where they'd be towed back to the sawmills at Strahan.

As more of the trees were felled, the loggers had to go further and further upstream to find fresh timber, dragging their rowing boats over narrows and up small tributaries. This extended the length of time they had to spend in the forest and meant they had to subsist on the most minimal rations. I found it incredible that people could live this way, but despite the hardships, it seems the loggers really enjoyed their existence. A video shown on the boat included interviews with some of the last loggers, reflecting fondly on their experiences.

TASMANIAN DEVILS

The next day, I packed up and headed for Cradle Mountain. It was dry when I left Strahan, but about twenty miles into the trip the rain started. At Rosebery, I stopped to have a cup of tea and warm up, and bumped into a lady I'd met in the Hobart YHA, Julie. She'd just spent three days at Cradle Mountain and said the fog hadn't lifted the whole time she was there and consequently she'd been unable to see the mountain.

This was not good news, but I thought I'd give it a shot all the same. By the time I got to the turn-off for Cradle

Mountain, the fog was coming in. Before long, it was so thick I had to pull over and stop as I could barely see in front of me. This did not bode well for future sightings. It was cold in the fog, so after a while I decided to brave it and carry on. By the time I made it to the National Park Visitors' Centre, I was cold and very wet.

I had booked an Alpine Hut in the campground and enquired where I might find this. To my dismay, I was informed it was just over the road, up the dirt track.

Oh my God, no! Not gravel *and* rain, I thought, but what could I do? I just had to do it. As I cautiously made my way to my hut, streams of water flowed down the track alongside me and I was surprised to find that the road surface was actually quite compacted under my tyres and was easier to ride than I'd imagined.

The hut was very basic, with three bunks in it. There was no electricity or heating, but it was a damn sight better than a tent so I quickly unloaded the bike and spent the rest of the afternoon in the camp kitchen, trying to dry off. A friendly retired couple from Geelong, Mark and Judith, came in and got a fire blazing. They were camping in a tent that looked more like a Port-a-Loo and had spent a few weeks touring around Tassie.

As the afternoon wore on and the rain continued to lash down, more and more people gathered in the kitchen – the only dry and warm building around. An English couple arrived who were camping in a tiny tent, which they assured me kept them dry, although it appeared to be swimming in a puddle of water, followed by a Canadian couple in a Wicked Campervan[4], which they'd grown quite fond of even though it didn't keep them warm at all.

The next morning, the fog lifted and we could see Cradle Mountain, a spectacular jagged set of peaks. I caught the park shuttle bus up to the start of the Dove Lake Circuit and spent a very pleasant couple of hours walking round the lake at the base of the mountain.

On the way back I stopped at the Tasmanian Devil Sanctuary and got to see my first Devils. They are about the size of a small dog, with black fur and a white spot or collar around the neck. The guide at the sanctuary, who had become "tolerated" by them, was even able to pick up one or two for us to stroke.

It would seem that Tasmanian Devils are quite misunderstood creatures. They are one of Australia's three carnivorous marsupials (the other two being Quolls, also bred at the sanctuary, and Tasmanian Tigers, now thought to be extinct[5]). A British General named them "Devils" on account of their tendency to have ferocious fights with each other and inflict deep gashes on their faces. However, the guide explained that this type of behaviour is only displayed if they feel threatened or, more commonly, as part of their struggle for dominance and breeding rights – a behaviour exhibited by most animals on earth.

Unfortunately, in the last twenty years, Tasmanian Devils have been plagued by a debilitating cancerous tumour called Devil Facial Tumour Disease (DFTD), which is spread through the scratches received in these fights.

According to the Devils@Cradle website[6], "DFTD is characterised by the development of ulcerated tumours around the jaws and head of the animal and is fatal as an individual usually starves to death in 3–5 months. It is thought that it affects 30–50% of wild Tasmanian Devils ... Numerous other threats have also beset the Devils over the last two centuries since Tasmania was colonised. It is unlikely that DFTD alone will result in the extinction of Tasmanian Devils but combined with the numerous threats already impacting on Devils their long term future is certainly not secure. Accordingly Devils are now listed as a vulnerable species under the threatened species act. Ten years ago they were considered common, abundant and secure!"

I spent all afternoon at the Devil sanctuary, observing them. There were several pens, containing adults, adolescents and babies. They were beautiful animals and I was alarmed to hear how endangered they'd become. Fortunately, this sanctuary is part of a national programme breeding uninfected Devils to re-introduce into the wild, and is contributing to the ongoing survival of these fascinating little creatures.

In the evening. Mark and Judith did a "loaves and fishes" dinner for everyone to use up the last of their fruit and veggies before returning to the mainland. It was a delicious meal and it was nice to spend more time with such a fun group of people.

That night, a storm of biblical proportions blew up. As I lay on my bunk I could hear the winds and rain thrash the walls and roof of my hut and I prayed I wouldn't need to get up and go to the loo during the night. I'd wrapped myself in several layers and made sure my feet were warm before I wiggled into my sleeping bag, but sleep was difficult as the hut shook with the force of the gale. At least I stayed warm and made it through the night without having to leave the hut.

Somewhat tired and groggy, the next morning I set off for Devonport and the ferry in the sleet. As I left the campsite, I noticed another motorbike in a bay near the exit that had a trailer attached to the back of the bike. The trailer converted into a pop up caravan. I had been impressed by the bike trailers I'd seen so far, but this really took the biscuit. If the owner had been around I'd have asked to have a look inside, but there was no sign of life so I had to continue on my way, my curiosity unsatisfied.

The road I had planned on taking was closed due to a fallen tree, so I followed the diversion signs and ended up travelling through some stunning country. What at first seemed to be dull, hilly farmlands became radiantly green as the sun came out and offered fabulous views over valleys below. As I descended to lower altitudes, I travelled through groves of tall, leafy trees and followed babbling streams sparkling in the sunlight. It was a joy to ride and a lovely parting memory of my time on the last inhabited island before Antarctica.

A TASTE OF HOLLYWOOD

I arrived at the ferry terminal at 1 pm, four hours before check-in. I was the first in the queue, but soon a truck and a van drove up next to me. The two drivers started chatting, so apart from nodding an acknowledgement to them, I carried on reading my book.

After an hour or so, the van driver wandered off and the truck driver pulled out a magazine called *Mega Trucks*. "Truck porn," he sniggered to me like a naughty schoolboy.

It made me laugh and we started talking. It turned out he and the van driver were part of the film crew for *The Hunter*, a film starring Wilhelm Dafoe and Sam Neil which had just been shot in Tasmania.

When the van driver returned, the pair of them went into a bit of a comedy act about the thank-you gift that had been given to all the crew. On most "shoots", the crew members get something cool like a jacket or T-shirt with the film name embroidered on it. On this occasion, they'd been given a tea towel. Not only did it not have the film name on it but it had a bunch of Tasmanian place names printed in black and white, some of which they hadn't even filmed at!

When check-in began, I was directed into a holding lane where all the bikes were being funnelled. Given that I'd been the first in the queue, it was a bit of a puzzle that I somehow ended up halfway down this lane.

As I dismounted, two of the WA boys I'd met on the way out pulled up behind me. Surprised and delighted to see them again, I bounded over and was introduced to their machines, Bessie and Gert. They were both on Harleys, which they'd rigged up with cameras on the handlebars, phone chargers, Sat Nav and two-way radios. I felt quite low-tech in comparison.

As I boarded the ferry, I passed Mark and Judith sitting in a car lane. We waved goodbye to each other and, once more, I was back in the hold of the ship. I never saw them again after that.

I'd had a fantastic time in Tasmania but, strangely, I found I was glad to be leaving. It was a beautiful island, full of contrasts – sunshine and sleet, sea and pastures, forests and flowers. I'd met many wonderful people and experienced much kindness, generosity and friendship, but somehow I was glad to be getting back to the mainland. Maybe it was just because it was so far from everywhere else. It felt very isolated, and those areas that had been populated were mostly small or medium-sized towns. Hobart was the only city – and even it seemed a little undeveloped.

The biggest benefit of being there, though, was that my riding had started to improve. Although I was still scared,

I'd started handling my load better, and being on roads that seemed more like those at home had lessened my anxiety and started to rebuild my confidence. It felt as though I'd reached a turning point, and I was really glad I'd jettisoned the idea of buying a car.

Yes, it had been a great visit, but now I was ready to get back to the motherland and meet up with my new riding buddy, Nick. What on earth was that going to be like?

Chapter 10: North West Passage

NORTH BOUND

I arrived back in Melbourne at 6.30 am on Saturday 11 December 2010. The bike had been stuttering a bit on the way up to Cradle Mountain, so I'd called Raceway Suzuki from Tasmania and arranged for them to have a look at it and give it a quick service before I headed north to Canberra.

The journey from the ferry terminal to the bike shop should have been a straightforward, fifteen-minute blast up the Tullamarine Freeway, but I couldn't find my way onto it and ended up taking a 20 km detour via the Western Gate Freeway. It wasn't really a problem, though, as I still got there for 7.30 am and as the shop didn't open till 9 am, this gave me plenty of time.

Another guy turned up at 8 am and kept me company till the staff arrived and opened up. I met up with Lisa for breakfast while they serviced my bike. Luckily all was well, so I was back on the road for mid-morning.

Another bit of poor navigating added thirty minutes onto my attempt to find the road out of Melbourne to Albury, my next stop. If I'd bothered looking at the map before I set off, I'd have seen that Albury lies on the Hume Highway, the main road to Sydney, but I had it in my head it was on a road of its own. It was only when this road didn't materialise where I expected it to that I looked at the map and realised my mistake.

It was horrible coming out of Melbourne: strong winds, dark skies and heavy traffic on a three-lane highway, but once I got clear of the city limits it brightened up a bit, the traffic thinned and the remainder of the trip was quite pleasant.

HIGH PLAINS DRIFTER

After a night in the Albury/Wodonga Youth Hostel I continued up the Hume Highway to Canberra. It was a great ride – sunny skies, light winds and not too much traffic on the roads.

Since this is the main road between Melbourne and Sydney, I had always imagined it would be densely populated, but it was quite the opposite. I only passed through two towns the whole way to Canberra. (I later discovered that a series of by-passes has been built round all the towns, so that was why it was so deserted.)

The highway became the main street of the first town, Holbrook, which looked like something out of a Wild West movie. It was lined with buildings that reminded me of saloons and I felt I should be throwing my poncho over my shoulder, rolling a cigar from one corner of my mouth to the other and ordering some hard liquor.

As I rode through, I noticed the crowd of bikers from Sydney that I'd met in Tasmania – the ones who'd found my wallet – parked outside a café. But I was past them before it registered, so I missed the opportunity of stopping and saying hello.

The other town, Tarcutta, consisted of a roadhouse and a few other small buildings. The front of the roadhouse's forecourt was full of trucks, with the petrol pumps accommodating an assortment of cars, utes and campervans. A crowd of young lads were trying to push each other off the bridge that spanned a small creek next to the entrance. I assumed they must be bored locals. As I was having some lunch, they kept coming in and out of the roadhouse, and when I was getting ready to leave they all piled into two utes, each pulling a fancy race car. They disappeared ahead of me in a cloud of dust.

Canberra sits at an altitude of about 2,000 ft (600 metres), so the road gradually rises up into the hills through great high plains of farmlands. It seemed to be mostly wheat but, unusually, a few fields were filled with tall purple thistles, reminding me of home.

There had been a lot of flooding in the previous couple of months and many fields were filled with large pools of water. As I got to Gundagai, I saw a whole valley swamped by flood waters and noticed that the junction with the Sturt Highway to the west was closed. This was the route I thought Nick and I would take to Adelaide and I was a bit concerned about whether we'd be able to make our way over there. But as there seemed to be several alternatives we could take I didn't worry about it unduly.

It took me until 4 pm to get to Canberra, so I had plenty of time to consider the subtleties of riding a motorcycle on a major highway. I discovered that truck drivers really don't like you overtaking them on hills. If you do, they come hurtling up behind you on the downhill stretch and practically run you off the road.

You can also receive quite a battering from all the insects that fly into you. I was hit so hard by one that I half expected to see a dart sticking out of my kneecap when I looked down. I also discovered that if I leaned forward over the tank, then I didn't have to grip the accelerator so hard and hence I could un-cramp my right hand.

I left the Hume Highway just after Yass and joined the Barton Highway into Canberra. I hadn't got very far when I noticed the two sets of boy racers, pulled over at the side of the road with the bonnet up and lots of head-scratching going on as they peered into the engine. I rode on by, relieved I'd taken out breakdown cover sometime earlier.

TWO'S COMPANY

When I got to Canberra, I checked into the YHA, did my usual weight-lifting routine with my luggage up to my room, had a shower and then called Nick.

We met up that evening. He turned out to be something of an Italian stallion of a guy – dark, brooding looks, a slim, fit build – and unexpectedly bashful. He had brought his motorcycle atlas along and, when I told him about the Sturt being closed, he worked out another, much more interesting route that would head across country on lots of small back roads.

We left Canberra the next morning and rode back along the Hume Highway to Gundagai, where we picked up the first of these back roads and started making our way west, across to Wagga Wagga. We stopped in a small village for a cup of tea and I nearly sprayed mine all over Nick when I accidently put salt in it instead of sugar. I thought this was hilarious but he didn't seem to find it quite as funny.

From there, it was a glorious ride through sparsely populated, undulating hillsides and farmland, with only the very occasional small township. Nick had been reading my blog and knew about my fear of gravel, so when we hit an area of this quite early on, he stopped to see what to do. As there were a few cars behind me, it was going to be harder for me to stop safely than to continue, so I just rode right over it, to both our surprise.

Later, the road was closed due to flooding and we were diverted through many more back roads. After a while, the diversion signs ran out and we had no idea where we were. Through some remarkable guesswork, Nick managed to navigate us back to the main highway and into Wagga Wagga. A huge section of land bordering the approach road was under water and I wondered if things would get worse or better as we went further west. The town centre had not been inundated, though, and we managed to find a pleasant little campsite and set up camp.

It had been a very hot day and, as the campsite had a swimming pool, I was dying to throw myself in and cool off. The trouble was, this meant exposing my somewhat oversized proportions to this handsome stranger and I really wasn't very keen to do that. Eventually, the need for cooling outweighed the need for modesty and I changed into my swimsuit, wrapped myself in a sarong and plunged into the refreshing waters. I was surprised and relieved to notice that Nick seemed just as body conscious as me, as he dithered about taking his T-shirt off and reluctantly followed me in.

Nick had been bragging about the tiny amount of luggage he'd brought with him, which he attributed to the fact that he had a "houchie" instead of a tent. A houchie is a tarpaulin with a poncho strung up above it. However, when the mosquitoes started coming out it began to look as if this might not be quite such a good idea. I suggested that he might like to share my tent instead, but he insisted on using the houchie.

Later, I couldn't help laughing when, barely five minutes after we'd gone to bed, I heard him saying, "Jill ...?" So it turned out that my one-man tent could actually take two people.

Now although I can appreciate a good-looking man when I see one, it doesn't necessarily mean I'll be attracted to him. And this was the case with Nick. He was definitely very easy on the eye but there wasn't really any chemistry between us.

Having said that, when a hunk of half-naked Italian muscle lies down next to you and it's been three years since you last had any, it's hard not to think amorous thoughts. Nonetheless, I have two rules I operate by when it comes to men. Firstly, *no married men* (even if they are separated) and secondly, *the man must make the first move*. And, as in this case no move was made, I did my best to push any wicked thoughts I might have been having to the back of my mind and concentrated my full attention on going to sleep.

Nick never explained why he wanted to ride with me and I never asked. He had recently separated from his wife, so I figured he either wanted some time out, was having a mid-life crisis, was looking for a fling with a foreign stranger or just fancied having a bit of a motorcycle adventure. Whatever the reason, it was clear by the second day that either I, or the trip, was not meeting his expectations. He started talking about how much he was missing his sons and I felt he was trying to pave the way for an imminent departure.

Nevertheless, he continued to guide me through the back roads of New South Wales. There were huge plagues of locusts everywhere (they were now much bigger than the tiny hatchlings I'd seen in Lake Boga – definitely stripping size) and we both ended up covered in insect splatter as we rode through the swarms. At one point, I nearly drove off the road when one of them got under my visor and started buzzing around in front of my face. By the time we reached Finley, the town centre was so thick with them that it felt like we'd ridden into a snow storm.

The day before, Nick had commented that I tended to lose speed in the bends, so I made a concerted effort to keep up with him and discovered that if you keep your power up and lean into the bends, you don't lose any speed.

Now I know this might seem pretty obvious to most bike riders, but I'd never really got the hang of leaning. Every part of my being resisted.

The logic of taking a large, heavy object and leaning it on its side just screams *fall over* to me. I prefer to slow down and engine-brake through the bends. I think the part of the equation I was missing was the bit about keeping the power on when you're leaning. I'm sure there's some sort of law about centrifugal forces that ensures you stay upright, but, up until now, my body wasn't buying it. However, following Nick through all the twists and turns forced me to give it a go and despite all logic to the contrary, it worked.

Just as I was busy congratulating myself on my new-found skill, we came riding into a series of floods. The first couple were okay, but when Nick dropped down a pothole and barely made it through to the other side we really had to pick our way very carefully. I think we both felt we'd earned our "river crossing endorsement" at the end of it.

MEGA BITES

We camped at Deniliquin that night. As we were preparing camp, I could tell Nick was a bit withdrawn and decided to give him some space and go for a walk.

As I was coming back to the campsite about an hour and a half later, he was on his way out to find me. There was a seat nearby so we sat down and had a bit of a chat.

"How you doing?" I asked.

"Oh, I'm all right," he replied dejectedly.

"Are you wanting to go back and be with your boys? I enquired.

"Yeah. You know, I haven't seen them much this year, and it feels like I should be with them rather than running around the country on a bike. But I don't want to leave you on your own either. I mean I said I'd come with you to Adelaide and we're not even half way there yet."

"Hey, don't worry about me," I said. "I was going to have to go this way anyway, so don't feel you're abandoning me. It's been great having you come along this far, but please don't feel bad about wanting to spend time with your sons."

"Thanks," he replied. "I think I'll sleep on it and decide in the morning."

Before we left Wagga Wagga, Nick had bought a mosquito net to hang under his houchie. However, he couldn't find a way to string it up, so he slept at Motel Maden again that night. Ironically, I was the one who ended up being eaten alive by mossies, while he never got a single bite.

The next morning I accidently walked into a spider's web and went completely berserk, which Nick found quite amusing. Not long after, I found a huge spider on my boot and had a girlie screaming fit. Any hopes I'd had of being viewed as a tough biker chick went down the toilet as Nick came to my aid and disposed of it.

As we were packing up, Nick decided he would, indeed, start making his way back to Canberra. I was sad to see him go as I'd really enjoyed his company and felt my riding had improved greatly by following him.

We parted ways at Barham and I could feel the tears prick my eyes as I rode off alone to rejoin the Murray Valley Highway to Swan Hill. I was generally quite happy riding by myself, but I was useless at goodbyes and always found it hard to leave people behind, especially when I liked them. Although there hadn't been any attraction between us, Nick had a caring sort of way about him and I'd enjoyed being cared for by him.

He was obviously a much better rider than I was, but he lowered his speed so that I could keep up, he paid for a tank of fuel for me, he lent me cash when I ran out, he bought me a pair of flip-flops for no reason other than that he thought I might need them, and he never tried to force his views on me when a decision had to be made. So, although I'd been quite apprehensive about having him along, I greatly appreciated all these qualities in him and felt sad riding off that day.

The skies had been darkening all morning and, as the road levelled out to give a panoramic view of the open plain, I was treated to a spectacular lightning storm. It was so impressive I pulled the bike over to the side of the road and watched as huge rods of light shot down to the ground below.

The Murray Valley Highway was the road I'd taken south to Melbourne after my house-sit in Lake Boga, so it meant passing it again on my way north-west. I couldn't resist turning off and taking a quick run up to the house I'd looked after. Nobody was about, but it was good to see the place again.

I then set course for Mildura. Beyond Swan Hill, the orchards and vineyards gave way to barren scrubland. I stopped at Boundary Bend, a town that seemed to consist of just a roadhouse and the attached caravan park, and was surprised to see that the Murray River had burst its banks and was almost up to the edge of the road. Fast-flowing, muddy waters swamped picnic tables in the adjoining park where the "bend" of the river had created a lagoon. Clearly a lot more water had fallen in this area since I was in Lake Boga six weeks earlier.

Mildura seemed to be full of motels so I stopped at the tourist information office to see which one would be cheap but still nice and have a swimming pool. They recommended one across the road and I booked in, had a swim and smothered myself from head to toe in sting-relieving ointment, to try and stop the itching of my mossie bites.

NEWS FROM HOME

Because Nick and I had been incommunicado for the last few days, I hadn't been able to check my email. As soon as I got settled in my motel room, I hooked up to the local Wi-Fi and re-established contact with the world. And there it was – the email everyone dreads. "Your Dad".

It was from my step-mother, Sybil, saying that my dad had had a stroke and was in hospital.

I felt sick. I immediately phoned home and spoke to Sybil. She assured me it had just been a mild stroke and only his speech had been affected. Luckily there was no paralysis and his limbs were still working – but it was still a stroke and the news left me in quite a state.

My dad had always been a very fit and healthy man. Apart from having the pacemaker fitted and a bad knee injury a few years earlier, he'd never really had anything wrong with him (or not that I knew about).

He was a scientist and keen mountaineer and had been largely responsible for my interest in travelling. When we were growing up, we travelled all over Europe with him and my mum, as they took us on holidays to various mountain ranges. His work had taken us to America on two occasions: a two-year stint in New York when I was three years old and a one-year stay in Baltimore when I was fourteen, so I guess I had viewed him as a bit of an invincible adventurer.

We'd had our ups and downs over the years, as most parents/children do, but before I left we seemed to have reached a pretty good place with each other and the news left me terribly torn. I didn't know what to do. Should I catch the next plane home or wait and see what happened? I'd only been on the go for three and a half months and I had commitments to keep in the form of house-sits.

I texted Nick and Lisa, who both sent messages of support, but ultimately I had to make up my own mind. In the end, I decided not to make any decisions until the consultant caring for my dad had given his full diagnosis.

WIND

I stayed two nights in Mildura. As soon as I rode in, I felt it was perhaps a bit of a rough town and, when I saw a guy being pinned to the ground by six police officers, my suspicions were confirmed. Although it was great not to have to contend with the mossies again and to have some time to rest and think about my options, I was glad to leave.

The ride from Mildura to Adelaide started off well – huge prairies of wheat interspersed with massive citrus orchards. Once again, I found myself pulling up at the side of the road to take it all in. But as soon as I hit the Barossa Valley, the wind really got up. I was having to bank the bike right over just to stay on the road.

The trouble with this technique is that, if the wind suddenly stops blowing, there's a good chance you won't be able to pull the bike upright again quickly enough and it will drop onto the road, spilling you across it. At one point, I pulled out to overtake a truck but had to give up as the combination of the tailwind from the truck and the crosswind on the carriageway meant I almost became detached from the bike – I could actually feel myself being lifted off the seat. As my accelerator hand had been cramping, I'd been making a conscious effort to loosen my grip on the handlebars when I set off, but the winds made it impossible to keep it up and by the time I got to Adelaide my fingers were numb and I was worried I'd inflicted some permanent nerve damage on my hand.

As soon as I pulled into the YHA in Adelaide, I met a young American lad, Dave, who was trail-biking round eastern Oz. He was highly entertaining and I spent the whole evening exchanging stories with him.

My room-mate, Robin, also an American, was really interesting, too. She had just spent two months sailing across the Pacific on a yacht.

"My God, didn't it scare you when you lost sight of land and only had ocean all around you?" I asked.

In reply, she said her thoughts would cycle through the following sequence: "What should I make for breakfast, when's my next watch, what's the weather forecast, *we're all going to die*, what should I make for lunch, when's my next watch, what's the weather forecast, *we're all going to die...*" and that she couldn't let herself get stuck on any one thought for too long.

Laughing, I agreed. I'd had similar thoughts on the prawn trawler.

KARMA

On returning to the hostel in Adelaide I discovered that there was only one decent mug left. For the four days I stayed there I hid this in the kitchen each time I'd used it. On my final morning I came down for breakfast to find that someone had stolen my milk. If this isn't karmic payback for such petty selfishness, then I don't know what is.

DIVIDED LOYALTIES

During my time in Adelaide I got news that the consultant felt that my dad's condition was not life-threatening and that he was starting to show signs of recovery. This, combined with the fact that I was due to start my house-sit in Whyalla in a few days' time and didn't want to let the owner down, meant that I felt able to decide to continue with my trip, although I would monitor my dad's situation closely.

SIGHT SEEING

I left Adelaide on Tuesday 21 December and rode round to Whyalla – another 400 km run. It took forever. I kept stopping to look at the sights or to give my bum a rest.

Despite feeling more confident on the bike after my times in Tassie and with Nick, now that I was on my own again I found the weight of my luggage was still influencing my every move. Should I stop and look at that spectacular pink lake? No, because the car park was made of gravel and I might skid. Should I try and overtake that truck? No, because I might not have enough power to get past. Should I go for a wander around the town? No, because someone might steal my gear.

Port Wakefield was the first major junction I came to after leaving Adelaide and seemed to mark the start of Road Train country. Thereafter, these huge three-trailer long trucks seemed to be everywhere. Mostly they went along pretty quickly, so my main interaction with them was dealing with the tailwind off the ones passing me in the opposite direction; but at one point I got stuck right behind one. The driver politely drove onto the gravel verge to let me pass, but the combination of the dust and the appearance of another one coming towards me meant I had to slam my bike down a gear and screw it up to 120 km/h to make it by in time.

From Port Wakefield to Port Pirie it was mostly farmland, but at one point I passed an astonishing pink lake. And when I say "pink", I don't mean a hint of pink; this was the deep pink of a glowing sunset. There was a parking area at the start of the lake on the opposite side of the road, but it was gravel so I sailed on by, missing a fabulous photo opportunity as I didn't pass another stop for the remaining length of the lake. I suspect the pinkness was caused by some form of algae, but I had no way of finding out for sure.

During a stop at Port Pirie, I patted a gorgeous little dog. Its owner turned out to be a Brit who had immigrated to Perth and was looking for a house-sitter, so I gave him my details and availability and hoped I'd be able to look after his dog in Perth after I'd finished in Queensland. This would mean I'd get to ride across the Nullarbor on the way back to Melbourne (a must for any self-respecting motorcycle adventurer).

On my first trip to Australia twenty-one years earlier, Sue and I had taken the bus from Melbourne to Perth. It took three days and, next to the prawn trawling, was perhaps the most arduous travel experience I'd ever had. I can't say I remember any of it particularly clearly, but as I made my way along I was getting a very strong sense of déjà vu, especially when I reached the foot of the Flinders Ranges near Port Pirie.

A bit further on, I stopped in Port Germein to look at "the longest wooden jetty in Australia", but as the tide was out I couldn't really distinguish it from the mud flats surrounding it.

Port Augusta was my next stop. There is a huge steelworks there and it's also where the road splits – one arm going north to Alice Springs and Darwin, the other going west across the Nullarbor Desert to Perth. I took the westerly branch and, a few kilometres later, joined the Lincoln Highway south to Whyalla. Seeing as I was a couple of days early for my house-sit, I stopped in the Visitors' Centre and enquired where I might find a cheap hotel.

The mature lady behind the desk asked why I'd come to Whyalla for Christmas and I told her I was there to house-sit for someone. Apparently satisfied with this explanation, she rang through to a hotel and booked me in.

SOCIAL CALENDAR

After I'd dragged all my gear through the car park, up two flights of stairs and along a long corridor to my room three times, the owner of the hotel appeared and told me to head down to the wharf at ten in the morning, as this was when the fishing boats came in, usually followed by schools of dolphins.

I jumped on my bike at the appointed time and set off. Two guys on Triumph Rockets whizzed past me, and when I arrived at the wharf, I found them there. I wandered over and started chatting to them. There were no fishing boats in sight but on hearing of my desire to see dolphins they offered to take me out on their boat the following week.

Next I went off to meet the lady I'd be house-sitting for. She said I'd been invited to spend Boxing Day with her parents and then introduced me to her landlady, who said she'd arranged for me to spend Christmas Day with a former resident. So I'd barely been in Whyalla for twelve hours and already my diary was filling up.

REPRIEVE

The lady I'd be house-sitting for advised me that she'd now be home on 29 December, not 1 January as originally planned (provided her flight back wasn't cancelled – she was going to a part of Queensland that had been badly affected by the floods). This was really good news for me as it gave me an extra three days to make the trip to Queensland.

WHYALLA

Whyalla's strapline is "Where the Outback Meets the Sea" and I'd say this is a fairly accurate description. As I came down the Lincoln Highway from Port Augusta it felt as though I was entering very remote territory. There was absolutely nothing between there and Whyalla, apart from a giant pipeline that ran parallel with the road.

Whyalla is a strange town. The first thing you see as you approach are the enormous steelworks, which extend right down to the sea. There is a small town centre which leads round to the marina/wharf area at the south-eastern tip. The rest of the town spreads westwards from this point in a large wedge shape. It's mostly houses, with a few industrial estates and a large shopping precinct. The place is very spread out, so having your own transport is essential for getting around. I couldn't even go to the shops without taking my bike.

SHIP BUILDING

On the way into Whyalla, the first thing you see after the steelworks is the HMAS Whyalla – a warship sitting in a field overlooking the car park of the Visitors' Centre.

It's 2 km from the coast, so I was curious how it got there. I was quite surprised when I went into the Visitors' Centre to enquire and the young assistant said, "Ah, yes, you're the one who's house-sitting, aren't you?" I tell you, news travels fast in a small town.

Apparently, from 1947 until 1978, Whyalla had a thriving shipbuilding industry. This was the first ship built and, after 40-odd years of active service, it was sold back to Whyalla for $5,000 in 1988. It then cost another $500,600 to winch the thing into its current position.

STEEL MAKING

Since Whyalla is dominated by the massive steelworks, I couldn't be there and not have a look around. On the morning of Christmas Eve, I took a tour and discovered that steel is made from a combination of iron ore and other raw materials. These are shipped in from nearby mines at Iron Knob (and other places, not so nearby, like Japan). Coal is baked until it becomes coke and then used to fuel the massive blast furnace in which the raw materials are melted and mixed. A mixture of molten iron and waste materials leaves the furnace. The waste materials are deposited in giant crucibles while the molten iron is transported by rail, in special containers that keep it liquefied, to the steelmaking and casting plant where it is made into large steel bricks. These bricks are then melted down again (and combined with recycled steel to produce different grades) in the rolling mill, where they are made into steel rails. These go into the cooling ponds and, once cool, are stored in yards until they're ready to be delivered to customers.

The whole site is 1,000 hectares in area (I don't know what that is in real money, but it was miles and miles) and also incorporates the old shipyards.

I had no idea that steelmaking was such a massive-scale industry. It seems they run this plant on a very "clean" basis, but it's easy to see what a vast amount of energy is required to power it all, and difficult to say that steelmaking is an environmentally friendly process.

CHRISTMAS

I spent Christmas Day with a family whose mother used to live in the apartments I was based in. Before starting this trip, this would have been my worst nightmare – spending the day with a group of people I didn't know. But I was getting used to meeting new people and finding it much easier to engage in conversation. I was still a bit apprehensive, but as soon as I arrived they gave me a present and a drink and started asking me all about my travels. They were great fun and made me feel very welcome.

The mother and father, who seemed to be about my age, both had children from previous marriages who all seemed to get along very well. There were four sons and a daughter, ranging in ages from about twelve to their mid-twenties. A lot of larking about was going on and, at one point, one of the older sons was subjected to a rather radical haircut with a pair of barber's shears. Surprisingly, the final result looked a lot better than the original cut.

As the morning passed, various friends and relatives arrived, and at lunch time over twenty people all sat down to a massive Christmas dinner. A huge, long table had been laid out in the back garden under a permanent canopy, which provided some blessed relief from the unrelenting sun. It was about 35°C – the hottest Christmas I'd ever had.

The meal started with masses of fresh prawns. After that, trays of sliced turkey and beef were brought out, with bowls of vegetables and all the trimmings. It was a huge feast and I was really impressed with the unbridled generosity of my hosts.

I was sitting at the far end of the table, near a guy from Glasgow called Duncan, who worked at the steelworks. Although he'd been in Whyalla for many years, he hadn't lost any of the Glasgow accent or banter and, when I said I was a Partick Thistle fan, he asked me to marry him. Even though it was just a joke, it was nice to hear the words.

I left about six o'clock, laden down with gifts and enriched by the family's benevolence.

In the evening I finally managed to speak to my dad, who was now back at home. It was a great relief to talk to him and discover that he was making a good recovery and that his speech hadn't been affected too badly.

I then managed to speak to my mum, whose husband had recently been diagnosed with vascular dementia. My mum is an incredibly caring person who always puts other people's needs ahead of her own, but I could tell that even she was struggling to cope. Once again, I felt very torn about whether I should stay or go back home and try to help my parents.

On Boxing Day, I went to dinner at the parents of the lady I was house-sitting for. Again, great hospitality – but I felt the need to be on my own with my thoughts that day and left early. The next day, I got a Skype call from Alicia, one of my friends back home. It was great to speak to her and it really cheered me up.

I loved travelling by myself, but I really missed the closeness of old friends.

PANIC STATIONS

I'd been left in charge of a rabbit, two budgies and a pair of goldfish. The rabbit was gorgeous, with the softest fur I've ever touched, but it tended to keep itself to itself. The budgies were very boisterous, though. From the moment I took off their cover in the morning till the moment I put it back on in the evening, they would twitter away and chase each other around their cage. That is, until one day when they went very quiet.

One of the budgies had a tumour in its tummy which made it look as though it had a big beer belly hanging over its perch. I had been a bit worried about this when I first saw it, but the owner said it didn't seem to be causing any problems.

But when they went quiet and I looked over, the one with the tumour had its head resting on the shoulder of the other one and seemed to be breathing very heavily.

Oh my God, don't die, I thought. *Please don't die.*

They just sat there, for what seemed like an eternity. "Please don't die," I kept saying. "Please don't die."

Then the budgies moved and slowly started tweeting again. I let out a huge sigh of relief, but I watched them very closely after that. I texted the owner to let her know what had happened and she said she'd been quite worried about the one with the tumour, too. Luckily they both returned to their former noisy selves and were still alive and kicking by the time the owner returned – but it had been a heart-stopping moment for me.

BUSH TELEGRAPH

The temperature had been rising in Whyalla and was forecast to get up to 45°C within the next week (a warm front was moving in from Western Australia), so I spent most of my remaining time there indoors, with the air conditioning on.

The boat trip with the two bikers never materialised, but one day I decided to go out and see the sights on my bike. I ran into another biker, who took great interest in my trip and told me all about the bike he was riding, an old Suzuki, which he'd just rebuilt.

The next day, I was out cleaning my bike when my downstairs neighbour who I hadn't met before, came out. Without a word of introduction, he announced, "My mate was talking to you yesterday."

It turned out that the biker I'd met and this neighbour worked together and, as I'd already discovered, the bush telegraph was obviously alive and kicking in Whyalla.

Despite more massive flooding in Queensland, the lady I was house-sitting for returned, as planned, on Wednesday 29 December. Once again, I had piled all my things onto my bike in order to get away as soon as possible after she returned.

At some point between Tasmania and Whyalla, I'd acquired enough stuff to force me to take my backpack out of my former bike-gear bag and strap it on top of everything else instead. This meant my tower of luggage was, once again, gaining height. As I was loading everything up, the downstairs neighbour came out again, with a friend in tow this time.

The pair of them proceeded to analyse my load and advise me how easy it would be to develop a "wobble" with that amount of luggage.

Really? I hadn't noticed.

OPENING UP

After my clinic closed down, I had withdrawn from the world. Oh sure, I continued to go to work each day and interact with the people around me, but emotionally I closed down. I didn't feel that anyone understood what I was going through, and my friends' offers of help never seemed to be what I needed, so I started shutting them out. I found it very difficult to engage with anyone on more than a superficial level. But being with Nick and all these kind people in Whyalla who knew nothing of my history but still welcomed me into their lives was really quite a healing experience and by the time I left Whyalla I was starting to feel happier and much more positive again. Which was just as well, since the next part of my journey would call upon every resource within me to get through it.

Chapter 11: Outback Odyssey

FLOOD PLAN

From September to November 2010, after years of drought, Australia experienced some of its worst flooding in living memory. The La Nina[7] weather phenomenon drenched north-eastern Queensland, producing its wettest spring on record. Heavy rains across south-eastern Australia affected large parts of New South Wales and Victoria, causing the floods Nick and I encountered as we made our way north-west.

On 25 December 2010, Tropical Cyclone Tasha hit near Cairns, bringing huge flooding with it. The floods forced mass evacuations of thousands of people from towns and cities. At least seventy towns and over 200,000 people were affected[8]. Three-quarters of the state of Queensland was declared a disaster zone. From Mackay in the north to Emerald in the east and Brisbane and the Lockyer Valley in the south, roads were impassable, airports were closed and supplies were cut off. Disaster was everywhere.

It was against this backdrop that I had to make my way from South Australia, through the floods, to Mount Molloy in northern Queensland, where my next house-sit was. I had been watching the disaster unfold on TV and figured there were two possible routes I could take that would avoid the majority of the flooding. The first was to go up the "red centre" via Alice Springs, then follow the Flinders Highway from Three Ways east across to Townsville and hope that the Bruce Highway would be passable to Cairns. The second was to go east from Port

Augusta to Cobar, via Broken Hill. At Cobar I could then join the Mitchell Highway north. This would also bring me out at the Flinders Highway but much further east, nearer Townsville. As the time I had was limited and this route was about 1,000 km shorter than the Alice Springs one (not to mention that it was now well into the Australian summer and the temperatures would be insufferable the closer I was to the centre), I decided to take the Mitchell Highway north. I knew I'd be skirting very close to the floods, but I felt sure this would be the best route.

Although I'd managed to gain three days to complete the trip (I now had twelve days instead of nine), I still had about 4,000 km to cover. I calculated that I'd need to ride about 400 km a day (the equivalent of riding the entire length of Scotland every day for ten days), with maybe two rest days, to make it by 9 January 2011.

Before the reprieve, I'd worked out that I'd need to make the following destinations in order to keep on target. I decided to keep to this schedule, to give myself plenty of time should storms or detours affect my progress:

Day 1:Whyalla – Broken Hill
Day 2:Broken Hill – Bourke
Day 3:Bourke – Charlesville
Day 4:Charlesville – Balcardine
Day 5:Balcardine – Emerald (if passable)
Day 6:Emerald – Charters Towers
Day 7:Charters Towers – Mount Molloy
(+ 2 rest days and time for detours)

As more floods were forecast and because I'd be travelling on my own, I made up my mind to check in with the local police at each port of call, so that someone would know where to send a search party if I didn't arrive.

TRAVEL PRECAUTIONS

While I was in Adelaide, I decided it was time to buy a decent map. On a number of occasions I'd seen a smallish Motorcycle Atlas for sale but I'd been too tight-fisted to buy it. However, Nick had a copy of it with him and, as it showed exactly which roads were sealed and which ones weren't (something I couldn't tell from my giant map of Australia), I decided to buy this, as I had absolutely no desire to inadvertently take a dirt track while I picked my way through the outback to Mount Molloy.

I also thought it would be wise to get a Mobile Broadband dongle so that I could update my blog as I travelled and let everyone back home know that I was still alive and kicking. I wasn't sure how many internet cafés there'd be in the outback or what level of coverage was available, so this seemed like a good way to guarantee a regular connection.

I was starting to get used to the cost of living in Australia now. As there was only going to be one youth hostel on my entire route north and I was a bit nervous about camping in the outback, I had to accept the fact that I'd need to start spending money on motels. I didn't have space to carry any food, so I also knew I'd need to buy my meals from roadhouses as I went along. Petrol was going to be a lot more expensive, too, once I got away from the main cities. But it didn't matter; I was going to have three months of free accommodation in Mount Molloy, so that would make up for the cost of the ride north.

Despite the intense heat, huge distances and treacherous weather conditions, I was really looking forward to this part of my trip. The tight deadline meant I wasn't going to be able to swan about as I'd done for most of my time so far, but that I'd really need to push myself. Plus, I'd be entering "the outback" – the unspoilt heart of this vast continent. I couldn't wait!

FLUIDS

RIDE STATISTICS: WEDNESDAY 29 DECEMBER 2010

From/To:	Whyalla – Broken Hill
Distance:	478 km
Depart:	11.00 am
Arrive:	6.30 pm
Total ride duration:	7.5 hours
Temperature:	37°C (at the Olary Hotel)

The first day, I almost cracked the 500 km in a day mark, but not quite. I left Whyalla at 11 am on Wednesday 29 December 2010 and it took me seven and a half hours to ride the 478 km to Broken Hill.

The reason the ride took so long was that I had to keep stopping. I was loaded down with gifts from the people in Whyalla which I couldn't carry, so the first stop was the Post Office, to send these to Mount Molloy. I also needed cash and therefore a trip to the bank was required. Here, I bumped into Duncan, the Glaswegian from Christmas Day. I had a short chat with him and was touched when he seemed quite sad to see me go. Then I had to decide what to do with my water bladder. The weather forecast was for temperatures in excess of 40°C, so keeping hydrated was going to be essential.

This was the first time I'd used the water bladder, so initially I had it inside my backpack on my back. But by the time I got to Port Augusta, 75 km later, it was very uncomfortable, so I stopped in a petrol station and strapped it on top of my luggage, with the tube hanging out so I could drink from it whenever I stopped.

Here, I also discovered the reviving properties of Gatorade. My *Birdsville* book had extolled the virtues of drinking isotonic drinks like Gatorade for replacing essential body salts and sugars. Riding up from Whyalla in the intense heat, I wasn't even aware of how much I was sweating. It seemed it was evaporating straight off my skin, leaving only a salty residue as a clue. Gulping down a couple of bottles of this stuff in the car park gave me an immediate hit and instantly brought my senses back to life.

Next I had to pick my way through a rather complicated route from Port Augusta through the Flinders Ranges, Wilmington, Orroroo and Peterborough to the Barrier Highway. I had to keep stopping to look at the map as I couldn't remember what place name to aim for next.

Then I ran out of fuel. Somehow, I managed to mistake a picture of a caravan on my map for one of a petrol pump, which meant that I expected Olary, the place in question, to have a service station.

It didn't. In fact, the only thing Olary had was a hotel and a few houses. The hotel looked a bit rough, but as I had no other choice, I went in. It was like a scene from *An American Werewolf in London* – the place fell silent as I walked in and all heads turned to face me.

There was an old man at the bar and a couple of other men behind it. It was dark and gloomy and for a moment

I had visions of disappearing without a trace. But when I blurted out how hot I was (it was 37°C at Olary) and how far I'd come, and asked, "Where is the petrol station?", this incited great amusement.

Sam, the hotel owner, told me, "There hasn't been a petrol station here in over 40 years."

"But there's one marked on my map," I said.

"Well, I don't know about that, but the last fuel was at Yunta."

"I know, I was there," I said. "I would have filled up, but I thought there was one here and that if I filled up here it would see me through to Broken Hill."

"Hmm," Sam mumbled, on seeing my consternation. "Wait here," he said, and disappeared.

A few minutes later, he returned with a flagon of fuel. "I keep a small supply round the back as there's always some idiot that misses the servo at Yunta and turns up here on empty."

"Er, thanks," I said, knowing I was one of the idiots to whom he was referring.

The final problem was that my accelerator hand kept cramping up and I had to stop every 40 km to give it a rest. By the time I made it to Broken Hill it was 6.30 pm.

Broken Hill seemed like a really interesting place, with lots of unusual street names like Bromide Street and Oxide Street – tributes, no doubt, to the town's mining history – and a big mine right in the centre of the town.

You can take tours around the mine but I'd arrived too late to do this. It is also home to the Headquarters of the Royal Flying Doctors Service and the School of the Air. I would have liked to spend more time there but, alas, my timetable did not permit.

While I was out exploring the town that evening, I passed the police station on the main street. As it was open, I thought this would be a good time to inform them of my plans. I told them I was going all the way to Mount Molloy but hoped to make it to Bourke the next day.

After they'd taken my details, I asked if they would send these through to Bourke and whether I should report to the police there when I arrived. They mumbled a few words along the lines that it would be a good idea, but something about the way they said it didn't fill me with confidence.

My accelerator hand was really starting to worry me. It had been cramping up continually throughout the day from holding the power on over almost 500 km, and I could feel that the outside of my palm down into my pinkie was going numb. I fell asleep that night massaging my right hand and wondering if there was any way I could stop it from cramping up so much. I was scared that this would become a real problem for me. If I had to keep stopping every 40 km to stretch my hand, it would severely hinder my progress.

CRUISE CONTROL

RIDE STATISTICS: THURSDAY 30 DECEMBER 2010

From/To:	BrokenHill – Cobar
Distance:	445.3 km
Depart:	10.00 am
Arrive:	5.00 pm
Total ride duration:	7 hours
Temperature:	40.7ºC (at the Wilcannia roadhouse)

Next morning I met a couple in the hostel who were on a bike. I told them about the problems I was having with my accelerator hand and the guy showed me a device he had, called a Cramp Buster. It had a round bit which clipped onto the accelerator and a flap which stuck out for your wrist to rest on. I could tell immediately that this would help me tremendously, so I shot over to the town's only bike shop and got one for myself.

The guy at the hostel had warned me that the Cramp Buster made it easy to over-rev the bike when you were going slowly, so it was best not to use it in the towns. As soon as I got out of Broken Hill, I pulled over and put it on. What a difference it made. You can rest your wrist on it, which holds the revs constant while the rest of your hand can have a break. It was as if some guardian angel had heard me the previous night and sent the solution along.

After my experience with the petrol the previous day and a warning from Sam that my fuel tank wasn't big enough to take me from the roadhouse at Wilcannia to Cobar, the second thing I did was buy a self-venting fuel can and fill it with fuel. (Lou had warned me that the heat would cause the fuel to expand, so to be sure to get a self-venting can if I needed to carry extra petrol.) However, I had to stop at three different petrol stations before I finally found a canister small enough to strap on top of everything else I was carrying. Surprisingly this was at the Little Topar roadhouse, a good 100 km from Broken Hill and in the middle of nowhere. None of the servos in Broken Hill had anything smaller than a twenty-five litre jerry can – fine for a four-wheel drive vehicle but a bit big for an already over-packed motorcycle.

After all this faffing about, several stops to adjust the Cramp Buster and a one-hour stop for a belated brekky, it took me till 2 pm to ride the 191 km from Broken Hill to Wilcannia. It was 40.7°C in the shade in Wilcannia and I was starting to feel weak.

After filling the tank, I parked the bike and knocked back two bottles of Powerade. A couple in a green Triumph Stag sports car pulled up next to me.

"God, it's hot," I exclaimed.

"Yeah," they agreed, "Where are you headed?"

As I began telling them my plans, I suddenly found myself gasping for breath and starting to shake.

"You need to go and stick your head under some cold water," the lady said. "Right now!"

I didn't need to be told twice and bolted for the toilets. I plunged my head (and everything else I could fit) under the tap. As soon as the water hit my face, I burst into tears as my body cried with the relief of being cooled down, and I realised how close I'd come to collapsing.

The Barrier Highway was the most desolate piece of road I'd ever travelled. It was bleak and barren and surrounded by gravel-strewn desert. It's so forsaken that it's where they filmed the post-apocalyptic thriller, *Mad Max*. It was utterly deserted, completely exposed, and there was only one tiny settlement marked on my map between Wilcannia and Cobar. I had no idea how I was going to make the remaining 260 km to Cobar with nowhere to stop and cool down.

By the time I came back out of the toilets I was a soggy mess, but at least I could speak again. As I made it back to my bike, a couple of very attractive guys on Harley-Davidsons pulled in. They filled their fuel tanks and then came over and parked their bikes next to mine.

They were only wearing jeans, T-shirts and leather waist-jackets with their club colours on them, but as soon as they dismounted they stripped to the waist and started pouring water over themselves. Even in my slightly delirious state, I couldn't help finding this a very appealing sight. I was amazed when they put just their waist-jackets back on (no T-shirts) to ride the next section.

"Hot? This is nothing," one of them said. "I've still got an ice-liner to wear if it gets really hot."

By this time I was starting to realise that my Shelltex jacket and trousers with full body armour and removable linings (which I had, by this time, removed) were, perhaps, not the best choice for such conditions. But I had no space left on the bike to carry them and I still didn't trust myself to ride without them, so I had to wear them. Besides, they'd been perfect when I was freezing my bits off in the south when I'd first arrived and it was going to be impossible to have the right gear for all conditions, so they'd seemed like the best choice when I was planning the trip.

We started talking. After the usual exchange of travel plans, they asked if I would like to ride with them to Cobar. God, I could have kissed them (in fact I did, later on).

"I have to warn you, I'm not a very fast rider," I said. "So if I fall behind, just go on."

"Well, we usually ride around the speed limit – can you keep up with that?" one of them asked.

This was 110 km/h in Australia, so I knew I could. "Yep, I should be able to manage that," I said and started up my engine. As we were about to pull off, I suddenly thought to ask, "What are your names?"

"I'm Glenn and this is John."

"I'm Jill," I said, shaking hands, and we set off.

I followed them for 200 of the remaining 260 km to Cobar. I was determined not to lose them in the blazing heat, so I rode harder than I'd ever ridden in my life. After an hour my bum was aching; after an hour and a half I thought I was going to scream with the pain. Fortunately, the Cramp Buster was doing its job and my hand wasn't stiffening up as much as before. It was also making it easier to keep my speed constant – I guess that's why they call it cruise control.

Then my tank flipped onto reserve and I had to pull over and fill up. I tried to attract the guys' attention, but Glenn seemed to be listening to music as he weaved all over the road and punched his arms in the air, and John appeared to be doing some sort of motorcycle yoga routine, so they disappeared off into the distance.

I was kind of relieved, as it gave me the chance to stretch out and ease the pressure on my throbbing behind. Besides, it was only another 60 km to Cobar, so I knew I'd be able to make it on my own.

When I pulled into the servo at Cobar half an hour later, they were waiting for me and I was able to thank them effusively for escorting me – I'd never have made it without them. They told me they were riding on to *Sydney* that night, a mere 600 km away. Given that they'd already done about 600 km, this meant they'd have covered 1,200 km by the end of the day. God, these guys were hardcore.

Needless to say, I didn't make it to Bourke that day. I knew I wouldn't, as soon as I rode into Cobar. But I'd survived the hottest conditions I had ever ridden in, so I was just happy to be alive and only 100 km or so behind schedule.

That evening, at the motel I'd carefully selected as it had the least amount of gravel in its forecourt, I got talking to the man in the room next to me. He rode bikes too, and did the usual inspection of my bike that bikers do and pointed out that my front tyre was bald.

Oh Lord, I thought. That's all I need – 4,000 km of outback riding and the one thing that could keep me attached to the road has the gripping qualities of a slab of butter.

When I walked into the town centre to find some dinner, I noticed there was a huge bike shop at the end of the street. Thank God, I thought, but my hopes were dashed when a notice stated they were going to be shut for the next two weeks for the New Year's holidays. Still, I hadn't realised the tyre was bald and had made it fine up to this point, so, like all responsible road users, I decided just to ignore it and carry on.

AIR CONDITIONING

RIDE STATISTICS: FRIDAY 31 DECEMBER 2010

From/To:	Cobar – Cunnamulla
Distance:	406.7 km
Depart:	9.30 am
Arrive:	4.00 pm
Total ride duration:	6.5 hours
Temperature:	40°C (at the Enngonia Hotel)

The next day, I thought I'd try a new strategy for combating the heat – a wet T-shirt. This had worked quite well from Wilcannia and I remembered reading in my *Adventure Riding Techniques* guide (by Robert Wicks and Greg Baker) before I'd left that this would help. So I ran my T-shirt under the tap before leaving the motel and wore it under my jacket. This proved to be remarkably effective and kept my body temperature to a more acceptable level.

I made sure I stopped every hour or so to drink and re-soak my T-shirt. As a result, the ride up the Kidman Way north from Cobar to Bourke was a real delight. I'd been dreading doing this road. Looking at my map, it wasn't even classified as a highway and I was afraid it was going to be a gravel track. I was greatly relieved to discover it was sealed. In fact, it was a superb piece of road, with an unbroken surface and stunning scenery, but there wasn't a single town along the entire 161 km length of it.

Everything was green and lush and I even saw a flock (?) of emus and several herds of goats (one of which I narrowly missed riding right into). Plus, I encountered my first flood waters on this part of the journey. Deep gutters at the side of the road were full of water and I hoped it wouldn't get any worse as I made my way north.

By late morning I'd made it to Bourke, where I stopped – partly so that I could have lunch but mostly because it meant I could now say I'd officially been to "the back of Bourke" – an Aussie expression meaning "the back of beyond". I also stopped there so I could let the police know I was still alive, albeit half a day late – only to find they weren't even expecting me. Broken Hill hadn't told them I was coming. I was a bit dismayed by this, but proceeded to give the lady behind the counter my details, in the hope that they would let my next destination know I was coming.

Leaving Bourke, I crossed a river which was so swollen with flood waters it was nearly up to the deck of the bridge. Further on, at Enngonia, the verges at the side of the road were, again, deep with water. It seemed the flooding was getting worse rather than better and I hoped I would make it through.

It was glorious riding, though. Long, empty roads with hardly any other vehicles meant I could relax and enjoy the breathtaking scenery around me. Vast expanses of bush spread for miles at either side. Occasionally I'd see a set of gates and a dirt track disappearing off into the distance, which seemed to indicate there was a cattle station nearby, but I never saw one. And sometimes I'd see herds of cattle near the roadside, but I'd never see farmers out herding them.

It was beautiful, though – the colours, the wildlife, the smells. Though the smells weren't always so good. Road kill is a frequent occurrence and often I'd smell it long before I saw it.

I was aiming for Barringun that day, just over the Queensland border, but as I'd reached it by early afternoon and as it was literally a two-building town, I decided to continue to Cunnamulla. The Mitchell Highway (which I joined at Bourke) was a good road but had no stopping places on it, so, about 60 km out of Cunnamulla I had to make an emergency roadside stop when all the Gatorade started filtering through. You know, it's just typical – I hadn't seen another vehicle for miles and then, as soon as I had to pull over and bare my all, one comes along. Fortunately, I just managed to conclude my business before it arrived.

A few kilometres on, there was a sign saying "Water Over Road". It turned out it wasn't all over the road and was, again, confined to the verges, but when I arrived in Cunnamulla, the girl in the bakery said that there was no bread as everyone was panic buying because the floods were due.

The forecast for the next week was actually for good weather, but now the flood waters in northern and eastern Queensland had started making their way over to where I was. At lunchtime, the police in Bourke said the road was passable to St George (a town about 300 km due east), but the bakery girl said they expected it to be cut off by that night. So I planned to try and outrun the flood waters by heading north-west the next day.

I figured that if I left early in the morning, I'd make it to Charleville, and from there I could either continue northwards to Barcaldine or go west to Windorah then north to Longreach on back roads. The latter option would add a huge detour onto my route, but it would be better than getting caught in the floods.

After the trip to the bakery, I went to check in with the police. This time, the police station wasn't even open and had a sign on it saying it would be closed until after the New Year, so I decided to abandon reporting my progress to them. By this stage I was updating my blog daily, as I knew my dad was worried about me (because of all the news reports at home about the floods). I knew that, between my friends in Australia and family back home, people were looking out for me and that if I didn't update the blog when expected, they'd raise the alarm and send out a search party.

That night, New Year's Eve, out of the three possible choices I found myself stuck in a grotty, north-facing, sweltering motel room in Cunnamulla. I had wanted to be within walking distance of the town centre, so I'd chosen the motel nearest it, but it turned out to be really shabby and even with the air conditioner on full blast it was like being in a sauna. Quite a contrast to the freezing alternative I usually had to deal with in Scotland at New Year.

OUTBACK MARATHON

RIDE STATISTICS: SATURDAY 1 JANUARY 2011

From/To:	Cunnamulla – Barcaldine
Distance:	674.6 km
Depart:	6.00 am
Arrive:	4.30 pm
Total ride duration:	10.5 hours
Temperature:	don't know but still very hot

I spent New Year's Day doing the biggest ride of my life – ten and a half hours and 674.6 km in the scorching Aussie outback. To put this into perspective, that's the equivalent of riding from Glasgow to London with someone firing a blowtorch in your face for the entire duration of the trip. But I made it to Barcaldine – *woohoo!* I was determined to get there that day so that the spreading flood waters (or more rain) didn't cause the road to be closed off before I got through.

I got up at 5 am and was on the road by 6 am. This was definitely the best time of day to ride. It was still quite cool, with the rising sun bringing out the landscape's vibrant colours. Plus, there were loads of animals about at this time. I saw kangaroos, emus, cows, birds of prey, and even a wild boar crossing the road ahead of me. Most of the animals wait until you get up close to them and then run out in front of you. I practically chased four young emus up the road at one point.

What seemed to be an abandoned railway line ran alongside the road. After an hour or so I got to a pretty little town called Wyandra, which had a row of wooden houses and a general store. I turned off the road, crossed the railway line and had a look around.

The store was closed so I continued past it and turned into a street that had a war memorial and a set of old fashioned red and blue petrol pumps with plastic shells on top of them. As it was only about seven in the morning, I couldn't tell if this was a working petrol station which hadn't opened yet or was just a vestige from a bygone business.

The light from the rising sun made the grass surrounding the village seem very green and lush and I found the whole place utterly enchanting.

The cooler temperature also made it much easier to cover the distances. By 8.30 am, I'd arrived in Charleville. The lady at the servo called the police for me and confirmed that the road from there to Augathella was closed, which meant I had to do a 100 km detour along the Warrego Highway to Morven, where I joined the Landsborough Highway, which took me north again to Augathella. In effect, I did two sides of a triangle instead of just one.

The Landsborough Highway was a really bad road to ride. It was strewn with potholes and had long, continuous waves of bumps. It was like riding on a rollercoaster and on several occasions I became airborne as I hit a bump too hard.

From Augathella it was a straight run up the Landsborough Highway to Barcaldine, a mere 300 km away. It's difficult to describe how hard it is to cover this kind of distance in such extreme heat, with no one to push you on but yourself. As the day went on and the heat increased, I needed to stop more often. I was trying to ride for an hour, then have a stop for fifteen minutes or so, then ride for another hour and so on, but after four days of sitting in a saddle that was starting to resemble a razor blade, my bum was hurting so much I found it harder and harder to keep up this routine. Occasionally I'd see a route marker detailing the distances to the next rest area or town, but at intervals like 87 or 138 km, this just made my heart sink. It could take even more than an hour to the next stopping point.

In Scotland, you get parking places every couple of miles, and seeing them pass this quickly makes the journey go by quite fast. But with this much space involved, it becomes a real trial to keep going. Not that stopping at the side of the road was an option. There wasn't a lot of traffic, but those vehicles that were on the road tended to be huge road trains, an encounter with which I'd never survive if it clipped me. So I sat in the saddle endlessly, waiting for the next rest area, trying to ignore the ever-increasing pain in my backside. Coming into Blackhall, I felt a series of acute stinging pops in my bum which made me practically scream with the pain.

But despite the pain and exhaustion, I was having the time of my life. As I rode along, I couldn't help notice the dramatic environment around me – the big skies, the endless horizons, the radiant colours, the isolated communities, the fabulous wildlife. It was staggeringly beautiful and I felt so privileged to be able to experience it all.

I may still have been scared, but the stunning beauty around me was giving me something else to focus on. And I was loving every minute. I began to appreciate all I had – I had a fantastic bike that never gave me any trouble, I had everything I needed to do the trip (piled up behind me), I had people looking out for me and coming to my aid when I needed them and I had the health and inner strength to keep going despite the most extreme conditions. I felt profoundly grateful that I was able to experience it all.

At Blackhall, the last town before Barcaldine, the lady in the service station said part of the road had been washed away so to be really careful. As I'd been going for nine hours by this stage and was completely exhausted, I had no trouble heeding her advice and reduced my speed to 80–90 km/h.

Not long after I passed the place where my half of the road had been washed away, an ambulance went racing past with sirens and lights blaring. It took me another twenty minutes to get to where it was heading – the site of a terrible crash. I couldn't make out which way up the car was, but there was a road train at the side of the road (undamaged), so I imagined the car was trying to overtake it and misjudged things.

It brought it home to me how isolated I'd be if I had a crash: it must have taken at least half an hour for the ambulance to make it to the scene of this accident. If I went off the road, the scrub could hide a bike quite easily and, with no witnesses to mark the spot, I might never be found.

Despite my marathon ride, I arrived safely in Barcaldine. I pulled up to the Barcaldine Motel and was immediately swarmed by tiny white sand flies. I ran for cover in the motel's office and noticed the lady behind the desk physically recoil as I came in. As you can imagine, riding in 40+°C heat for ten hours in full motorcycle protective clothing leads one to sweat heavily. This, combined with the smell of my dank T-shirt, meant I was absolutely stinking.

I apologised profusely and promised to take a shower straightaway if she would just give me a room. This made her laugh and a room was duly granted.

The owner later informed me that someone had managed to get through from Townsville in the north-east, earlier in the day. As Emerald in the east was still under water and the road to it was closed, I decided to take the same route as the people mentioned, except in reverse, which was:

Barcaldine – Longreach – Winton – Hughenden

At Hugenden I'd be able to join the Flinders Highway, which would take me through to Charters Towers. From there, instead of going to Townsville and then joining the Bruce Highway to Cairns, I could take the Gregory Development Road to Mount Molloy. So I only had two to three more days' riding to go.

I wasn't sure whether I should continue riding the next day and try to make as much progress as possible while the weather was still good, or take the day off and recover. I had made it past the level of the worst flooding now, so I felt I could start to relax. But I'd been going hell for leather for so long, it felt as if it would be wrong to stop. In the end, though, I decided to have a break.

Barcaldine was a nice little town but the heat and the sand flies made it difficult to spend any time outdoors, so apart from a brief circuit of the town centre, I pretty much stayed in my room. This was fine, though – it turned out that the stinging pops of the previous day's ride had been huge blisters on my bum bursting, so it gave me time to cover them with antiseptic cream and take the pressure off.

Before I went to Tasmania, I'd figured that the best way to deal with the varying temperatures in Australia was to wear footless tights under my riding trousers. In the cooler areas like Tassie, they would keep me warm, and in the hotter areas, they would stop my riding trousers from sticking to my legs and make it more comfortable.

The "footless" element would mean I could wear them for several days before having to change them (I'd only have to change my socks), meaning I wouldn't have to carry too many pairs. What I hadn't realised was how sweaty they would get. Putting sweaty tights back on means the salt in them starts to rub – hence the blisters. Having said this, I'm sure the blisters would have been much worse if I'd had the riding-trousers sticking directly to my skin; but one way or the other, my bum was taking a real hiding.

ROAD TRAINS

RIDE STATISTICS: MONDAY 3 JANUARY 2011

From/To:	Balcardine – Hughenden
Distance:	480 km
Depart:	6.00 am
Arrive:	2.00 pm
Total ride duration:	8 hours
Temperature:	unbelievably hot!

I was back on the road at the crack of dawn the following day. Over the flat, endless plain to my right, there was a huge bank of dark clouds to the north. Although I was currently travelling west, at Longreach I'd turn north, so I hoped this wouldn't take me into a storm. I knocked off the first 100 km to Longreach by 7.30 am. I'd have liked to stop there, as the Qantas Museum of the Air is located in Longreach, but as it was hours before opening time (and a holiday Monday) there was no point in waiting around.

Barcaldine onwards saw the introduction of my first four-trailer road trains. As I came out of Longreach, I encountered four of them in a row and got swept violently all over the road. No matter how often it happened, it just didn't get any easier, dealing with the slipstreams of these giant juggernauts.

The early start meant I made good time to Winton, but the ride up the Kennedy Development Road to Hughenden – oh my God, I thought I wasn't going to make it. The heat was so intense. It was 214 km of single track, heavily rutted road, without a single stopping place to offer any shade. There were no signs of flooding whatsoever on this road – just acres of parched, sandy scrubland. The storm clouds I'd seen earlier seemed to have dispersed so there wasn't even a chance of a light soaking to cool me down. There was a small township at Corfield but, because of the holiday, the one building that looked like it might offer refreshment was shut.

I pulled over at the side of the road about six times to drink and soak myself in water. After about 150 km, I was jubilant when I rode into another small settlement called Stamford and discovered it had a roadhouse. But my spirits were quashed when I found that it, too, was closed. Thankfully it had an outside toilet block which was open, so I was able to soak myself with water again, but by the time I got to Hughenden, I was shaking like a leaf.

The man at the petrol station gave me a seat in his shady workshop and, as I tried to bring my uncontrollable shaking under control by guzzling down three bottles of Staminade, he popped his head round the corner and said, "I've opened up the shower for you, if you want to go and cool down." I have never been so grateful in all my life.

I was so exhausted, all I could manage to do was take off my jacket, trousers and boots. Everything else I just wore into the shower, where I again dissolved into a sobbing wreck. The heat was so draining, I felt physically and emotionally spent.

As I came back out, the owner said, "Feeling better now?"

"Yes," I mumbled weakly, but I wasn't really.

"Hmm," he said. "I was a bit worried about you. You looked like you had heatstroke coming on."

Although I made it to Hughenden by 2 pm and could have tried to do another 100 km or so, I figured I should quit while I was still alive. I asked the garage owner where to find a motel and he recommended one around the corner.

I was so grateful to him for all his help that when he asked what I did for a living and, on discovering I was a massage therapist, started complaining about the pain he was having in his back, I felt obliged to repay his kindness by offering him a treatment.

Now massage is a profession that has always been open to misinterpretation, so when he asked if he should bring some beer for me, it immediately got my defences up. I explained that that wouldn't be necessary but when he arrived at my hotel room that night and told me how pretty I looked, I really began to panic. I decided the only way to handle the situation was to be as professional as possible, so I ignored his compliment and delivered a thoroughly proficient treatment.

He was very respectful, though, and I felt bad when, at the end of the session, I rather hurriedly dispatched him from my room. However, in my somewhat exhausted and fragile state I didn't want to end up creating any situations that could be misconstrued.

WATER OVER ROAD

My plan for the next day was to ride east to Charters Towers and then take the Gregory Development Road north to Ravenshoe. But when I woke up the following morning and thought about having to do another Development Road[9] in the blistering heat, I almost didn't get up at all. I had really scared myself the day before and I didn't want to end up over-exposing myself again. So I prayed, "I'm going to need some help today, God."

Within a few minutes, it occurred to me that I should just ride as far as Charters Towers (250 km), and then do the Gregory Development Road the following morning while it was still cool.

Feeling a lot better with this plan, I set off. About 70 km outside Charters Towers, I saw the first sign for "Water Over Road". It was only over my side of the road, though, so I was able to pass it quite easily on the other side.

A few kilometres later, another sign warned of more "Water Over Road" and there, ahead of me, the road was completely submerged. A creek, swollen with flood waters, had burst its banks and created a small lake over the road. There were cars and trucks queued up on either side, with their owners wandering up and down trying to figure out if they could get across.

It was about 50 m wide and 30 cm deep, flowing quickly and had a strong current. The road was also full of potholes, so even though the trucks and some of the bigger cars managed to ford it, I decided not to. If I hit a rut and lost my balance, the current would flip me over in seconds and I'd be a goner.

A passing police patrol advised me to wait until it was down to 20 cm, so I figured the best thing to do was to turn back and get some breakfast at a nearby café, and see if the waters had receded at all on my return.

When I came back an hour later, all the cars had gone and I was the only one there. The depth indicator showed it was now 20 cm high but the current still felt too strong for me, so I decided to wait and see if it subsided anymore. I waited for about an hour in the blazing sun, splashing the flood waters over myself occasionally to keep cool and walking across from time to time to see if the current had lessened.

Then, just as I was thinking about how a truck driver ferried Ewan and Charlie's bikes over some rivers on the Road of Bones in *Long Way Round*, and how good it would be if that happened to me, a lovely man called Keith pulled up in his Land Cruiser ute and offered me a lift over. I couldn't believe it. He was tall and lean, had a rolled-up cigarette hanging from the corner of his mouth and wore an Akubra[10]. He reminded me a bit of Crocodile Dundee, without the crocodile clothing.

He was so masterful and took complete charge of the situation. He drove his ute onto a verge so that the ramp at the back wasn't too steep, and just walked my fully laden bike over to it as if it were a push bike.

We needed to unload it to get it up the ramp, after which I had to stand on the back of the ute and hold on to the bike for dear life so that it didn't topple over as we forded the creek. A couple of other guys helped us get it back off again at the other side. I gave Keith a huge hug at the end, which he seemed to appreciate even though I was still soaked in flood waters. I found it interesting how attractive I was finding every guy who stopped to rescue me.

I was so overcome with gratitude afterwards that I cried practically all the way into Charters Towers. I'd met some of the kindest, most helpful people here. They never made a fuss; they just assessed the situation, realised I needed help, and provided it.

Just outside Charters Towers I stopped at a service station for fuel. I guess I must have been there for about ten minutes when a guy on a Harley-Davidson rode in behind me. I looked at him, surprised, and asked, "Have you just come from Hughenden?"

"Yes," he replied.

"How did you get across the flood?"

I was astonished when he said he'd ridden right through it. He was only a few minutes behind me so it couldn't have gone down that much, but he wasn't heavily laden, so obviously it hadn't posed such a problem to him.

When I told him it had taken me five days to ride from Whyalla, he said, "Gee, you're slow – it's just taken me two days to ride from Adelaide."

This totally burst my bubble. All the bonhomie of earlier dissolved in an instant and I felt like a complete lightweight.

I spent the rest of the day trying to justify to myself all the reasons why I didn't have the same abilities as people born in Australia, who were used to the heat and the distances and had nice big, comfortable Harley-Davidsons (with minimal luggage) to keep them speeding along. I bet he didn't have blisters on his bum to show for his efforts.

In Charters Towers I found a charming old traditional hotel with gorgeous big verandahs and a cool afternoon breeze. The owner let me park my bike under a shelter in the back yard and then I had to lug all my stuff up to my room. By now, it was taking five trips to get everything off (and on) the bike – one for all my riding gear (which, because of the heat, I'd have to take off as soon as I stopped), one for my backpack and fuel canister, one for the bike-gear bag, one for the panniers and a final one for the top box. On top of a full day's riding in the sweltering heat, it was utterly draining, even if the bike was right outside the room.

Since leaving Whyalla, I'd been lucky and had always managed to get ground floor rooms with parking right outside the door, but in this case everything had to be carried from the bike to the hotel, up three flights of stairs and then along a long corridor to my room.

I was dripping with sweat by the time I'd finished. A cool shower later and I was out on the verandah, letting the wind blow away all my exasperation and marvelling at the huge storm clouds building in the distance.

ALMOST THERE

RIDE STATISTICS: WEDNESDAY 5 JANUARY 2011

From/To:	Charters Towers – Atherton
Distance:	502 km
Depart:	6.00 am
Arrive:	4.00 pm
Total ride duration:	10 hours
Temperature:	cooler but humid

I was almost there. I left a very humid Charters Towers at 6 am the next morning and took the Gregory Development Road up to Ravenshoe. As this goes up into higher ground it was actually quite cool, and this, combined with a much better road surface, made for a really enjoyable ride. The road was flanked with lush green bush and eucalyptus trees, and small herds of cattle would gather near the fences by the roadside.

When I stopped at the Bluewater Springs roadhouse for fuel and breakfast, I discovered that this used to be a big mining area, the development road having been built to get the ore out. As I continued along the road, I passed the entranceways to several mines which were still active, and had to deal with the usual whipping tailwinds from trucks hauling their output. No wonder the road had been resurfaced – there was money "in them thar hills".

Eventually the Gregory Development Road joined the Kennedy Highway. I saw a sign for the Undara Lava Tubes, a place I'd visited on my last trip to Australia, and then, as I came into Mount Garnet, I had a sudden, very strong sense of déjà vu as I crossed over a bridge and pulled into the roadhouse. It wasn't until I got to Innot Hot Springs that I realised I'd been on this road before – both on my first trip to Oz when Rod, Shane, a girl called Emma and I had all gone up to explore the Atherton Tablelands one weekend, and then on my last trip, when I'd gone this way to get to Undara.

I arrived in Ravenshoe by 1 pm, which put me in a bit of a quandary, as I couldn't decide if I should go to Cairns to get a new tyre for my bike (and where I could hang out for a few days before the house-sit was due to start) or continue inland along the Kennedy Highway directly to Mount Molloy. I asked the Tourist Information man and he said I could get the tyre replaced in Ravenshoe. However, when I arrived at the recommended place, it turned out they didn't stock tyres for motorbikes.

The man there said there was a bike shop in Atherton and to try there. Again, I was starting to feel shaky, so he let me sit down on an upturned crate in his garage and we whiled away the next half hour talking about the challenges of outback riding, as my body came back to life. One of the nice things about stopping in remote areas is that the pace of life is a lot slower and people aren't in the same hurry as they are in the cities. It was good to sit and chat and not feel that I was holding him up.

Feeling revived, I made my way to Atherton and found the bike shop. They had the right tyres and I arranged to take the bike back there in the morning before doing the final 100 km up to Mount Molloy.

Atherton is a harvest town, which meant that, although it had a couple of hostels, you could only stay in them if you were working on one of the nearby farms. I therefore had to go for one of the two hotels instead. As there were parking restrictions on the main street outside both hotels, I went for the one that had a car park at the back. The only trouble was, it meant I had to carry all my gear across the road, up a set of steps at the back, along a long walkway, through the restaurant, up two flights of very steep stairs and along another long corridor to my room. Multiply this by the usual five trips and add to it the fact that there was no air conditioning and you have one very hot, sweaty and exhausted rider.

I decided to have dinner in the hotel's restaurant that night. I ordered my food and the hostess suggested I might like to have a drink at the bar while I waited. As I hadn't had a drink since I left Melbourne, this seemed like a fine idea. I'd had a shower, washed my hair and put on a pretty dress, so I didn't have my usual helmet hair and sweaty T-shirt look going on and was actually looking quite nice for a change.

I wandered over and sat down on a stool. "A bottle of cider please," I said to the girl behind the bar. And as I sat there, sipping the cool amber nectar, an extraordinary thing happened. A handsome man came up and started talking to me.

Clearly he thought I was a prostitute, though, as he looked me up and down and said, "Er, do you come here often?"

But I didn't care; he was a man and he was talking to me. I politely put him right by saying, "No, I've just ridden up here from Whyalla on a motorbike."

This caught his attention and he started asking lots of questions about my trip.

Just as I was thinking: At last! This could be it – I've found the man of my dreams, he was joined by a large group of adults and children, who whisked him away to a distant table and I never saw him again. Still, it was nice to get a bit of male attention for a while.

OUTBACK RIDING

Riding in the outback was proving to be an incredible experience – extreme, but incredible. The vast expanse of space was jaw-dropping. I could go for hundreds of kilometres and hardly see another soul.

Early in the morning, the kangaroos and the emus would be out. The emus were quite difficult to spot, but sometimes I'd catch a movement out of the corner of my eye, and when I looked I'd see half a dozen long necks poking up over the long grasses. Sometimes I could be looking right at them without even seeing them; it was only when they moved that I'd notice them.

Every 200–300 km there'd be a large town, and when I say "large" I mean maybe with a population of a few thousand people. There'd be a handful of shops, a school and usually two or three hotels with bars or a motel or two. Often there would be some point of interest like a museum or an observatory, but I was always passing at the wrong time of day to be able to stop and see these attractions. In between the bigger towns, you might get the occasional little township with a few houses. You'd be lucky if there were any amenities, like a roadhouse or a general store.

The heat was the hardest thing to handle. I was riding in temperatures of over 40°C every day (and that was in the shade; out of the shade it was nearer 45°C). My early starts were making the morning shifts much more tolerable but the afternoon sessions were intense. Although the wet T-shirts and regular soakings were helping, the strain of spending upwards of eight hours in the unrelenting sun and the lack of shade was really wearing me out. At least the winds weren't as bad riding from south to north as they had been from east to west. Either they weren't as strong or it was just that headwinds were easier to deal with than crosswinds. The only trouble was, it was like riding in the Whyalla Blast Furnace – these were not cooling winds by any stretch of the imagination.

My days had started to take on a pattern. I'd be on the road by 6 am, ride for about 100 km, stop to give my bum a rest and stretch out my hand, and then carry on for another 100 km. About mid-morning, I'd stop for brunch at a roadhouse. Every town has a roadhouse: in fact, sometimes the roadhouse *is* the town, so it tends to be the heart of the community. You can get everything there from petrol to a cooked meal or your weekly groceries, and often even postal services and accommodation. Everyone knows everyone and it's always easy to walk in alone and soon have exchanged travel stories with half the people there. I loved this life.

I'd spend the rest of day riding, stopping occasionally to fill up the bike, cool off and relieve the pressure on the sores on my bum. The longer I was in the saddle, the more breaks I had to take, as the pain would become quite acute. By mid-afternoon I'd usually have made it to where I was going, so I'd find somewhere to stay, have a shower and find a place to have dinner. Before bed, I'd update my blog and review all the wonderful experiences I'd had. Then I'd do it all again the next day.

Despite all the hardships, though, I loved riding in the outback. It taught me that, no matter what else was going on – fear, anxiety, heat exhaustion, natural disasters – it is always possible to find joy and beauty around you, if you're prepared to look outside yourself. I spent hours marvelling at the country surrounding me, the subtle changes in colour as the sun made its way across the sky, the gentle shift in temperature as a clump of trees cast its shadow over the road, the twitching ears of kangaroos as they heard the sound of my engine approaching. It showed me how perfect nature is – how the animals only came out in the cooler hours of the day, how the birds would hitchhike lifts on the backs of strolling cattle, how parched deserts could be transformed into lush meadows after a heavy rain. It taught me how to enjoy myself, despite my fears, just as I had hoped I would learn, back in Adelaide.

I was in the lap of love in the outback – its magnificent beauty, its endless horizons, its wonderful, kind inhabitants. For me, it was a deeply spiritual place and I could completely understand why the native Aboriginal peoples treated this land with such reverence. Under such changeable skies, it's easy to see why people started believing in the Gods. Every time I'd been in need of help, it had been provided, and

I couldn't help but wonder if there wasn't a sacred force looking after me.

FINAL DESTINATION

I finally made it to Mount Molloy on Thursday 6 January 2011. It had taken eight days of riding and one rest day to do the 3,330 km from Whyalla, but I'd made it.

I was absolutely elated. I'd ridden from one side of Australia to the other, through the most extreme weather conditions I'd ever known and through some of the most remote country on earth. I felt completely vindicated – whatever the man at the service station in Charters Towers had said and despite all the warnings Lisa and Lou had given me about the perils of riding alone in the outback, I'd done it. At last I felt I was a bona fide motorcyclist. I may not have been fast; I may not have been pretty, but I'd done it. For me, it was the greatest achievement of my life.

Chapter 12: Tropical Turmoil

MOUNT MOLLOY

The last 100 km, from Atherton to Mount Molloy, was a beautiful ride. The road passed through the Atherton Tablelands, a mixture of rainforest and farmlands, weaving its way along the top of the Great Dividing Range[11]. Tight passes through the rainforest led up to open plains filled with fields of sugar cane, bananas, mangoes and other exotic fruits. The final 40 km from Mareeba returned to uncultivated bush encircling wide, open lakes nestled at the foot of rainforest-clad peaks.

Mount Molloy itself was a beautiful place. High up in the rainforests, it was a small town with one main street containing a pub/hotel, a café, a post office, a general store and two art galleries.

As I rode up and saw the house I was to be looking after I felt I'd truly arrived in paradise. It was a beautiful old Queenslander[12], complete with stilts and verandahs. From the outside, it looked absolutely beautiful with light paintwork and vibrant stained glass windows. It was sunny when I arrived but later that day there was the most almighty thunder storm. The sound of the rain hammering down on the tin roof and the energy of the storm was fantastic. I thought I was going to love it there. Little did I know what I was letting myself in for.

MYSTERIOUS MOTORCYCLE MISHAP

When I arrived in Mount Molloy I parked my bike outside the house with its rear wheel against the kerb and its nose pointing out into the street. I'd discovered early on in my motorcycling career that it's never a good idea to park a bike nose in to the kerb if there is any sort of slope or downwards camber, as the only way to get it back out again is to manually push it backwards and, if it's a steep hill and/or a heavy bike, this can be near-impossible. Parking it with its wheel against the kerb and its nose facing outwards means all you have to do is apply the power of the engine and drive off.

Therefore it was with great surprise that I returned from a tour of the village on my first day, to discover that the bike was now parked parallel to the kerb and slightly nose in. When I enquired of my hosts if they knew what had happened, they said they didn't. Upon closer inspection, I noticed that one of the mirrors had been knocked out of place, the tip of one of the handlebars was slightly bent and there were quite a few strange black marks over the front mudguards and forks. The most likely explanation was that someone had knocked it over, but no one was admitting to anything.

SETTLING IN

The first thing I did when I arrived was unpack. I had a room of my own and, as this was the first time in five months that I was going to be somewhere for more than a few weeks and I had enough space to put my stuff without it getting in anyone's way, I revelled in the joy of finding places to put everything. I couldn't wait to be left alone and be able to settle in properly.

As I'd arrived in Mount Molloy a few days early, the people I was house-sitting for used the time to introduce me to the community. On the Friday they took me to a local swimming hole (oh, the joy of being immersed in cold, refreshing water), followed by dinner at the pub, where I met many of the locals. On the Saturday, it was their son's twenty-first birthday so I spent the day helping them prepare the local hall for a big party that night, where I met most of the rest of the inhabitants of the town. Sunday was breakfast with the owner's mother, followed by lunch with her father.

CHARACTER FLAW

On the Monday, the owners left for their holiday and I headed down to the coast to get "orientated" at the owner's business. It turned out that she had a spa in one of the towns on the coast and part of the reason she had chosen me to be her house-sitter was because I was a massage therapist and she was hoping I'd help out at the spa.

When I was making my way back through the Atherton Tablelands on the way to Mount Molloy, the scenery reminded me of all the fantastic places there were to visit. I was really looking forward to spending my time exploring and revisiting these, but three months did seem like quite a lot of time to fill, so I'd half-heartedly agreed, suggesting that, perhaps, a couple of half-days a week might be all right. As my visa didn't allow me to work, we agreed these would be on a strictly voluntary basis.

When she then announced that she'd rostered me on for five full days a week, I was appalled. This seemed like a gross abuse of my goodwill and also left me feeling very nervous, as I knew I'd have difficulty proving I wasn't getting paid if someone from the Immigration Service turned up. I did manage to negotiate it down to four days, but I was still very put out and extremely uncomfortable about the whole arrangement. Of course, I could have said no, but she'd caught me off guard and, eager to create a good impression, I'd felt obliged to agree. But even though technically I wasn't doing anything wrong, I knew I'd left myself vulnerable.

When she said I'd need to buy a black T-shirt to wear as a uniform, it seemed like a bad omen. I hated wearing black. It drained all the colour out of my already-pale skin and sapped my spirit of energy. Granted, I had been wearing black motorcycle clothing throughout my trip, but I'd been able to brighten this up with different-coloured T-shirts. Having black next to my face was not a good look for me.

The owner also said she would "give" me some towels to use, but when she handed them over she said, "I usually charge people ten dollars a week to use these, but because I've not bought any food for the pets, I'll let you use them for free if you get the pet food."

The usual deal with house-sitting is that you get to stay in the house for free if you look after their pets and that everything required to fulfil this duty is provided. I was so taken aback by this sudden change of terms that I didn't know what to say and ended up agreeing again, because I was put on the spot. But it just deepened my sense of being taken advantage of. When I went to use the towels, they smelt so stale I couldn't use them anyway, and I ended up having to buy my own (as well as all the pet food).

These incidents, together with the massage I'd agreed to do in Hughenden, flagged up a character flaw I had – a tendency to people-please. In an effort to be seen as a good person, I'd ended up agreeing to do a number of things I didn't really want to do and opened myself to potential risk in the process. The simplest thing on all these occasions would have been to say, "Let me think about it," as that would have bought me some time to consider how I really felt about the requests, but instead I said nothing and just stewed inwardly. So I'd learnt a valuable lesson. My new mantra from now on would be: *Let me think about it, Let me think about it, Let me think about it.*

LITTLE HOUSE OF HORRORS

When I signed up for this house-sitting lark, I went out of my way to demonstrate to prospective house owners that I was a good, honest person and would neither trash their home nor harm their pets. It simply never occurred to me that house-sitting is a two-way street and that I should check out what I was taking on before getting involved.

After my orientation, I returned to the house and decided to blitz the kitchen. Dirty dishes had been left all over the counters, open bins lay under the shelves and plates of congealing food sat in the fridge. As a result, the kitchen had an ant infestation.

Five hours later, I'd scrubbed the fridge to within an inch of its life and removed all traces of food from every surface I could find. Apart from the cupboards, that is, which were full of cockroach and insect remains. These almost made me retch, so I piled all the things I needed into one clean space and decided never to open the other cupboards again.

The bathroom was in a similar state, with the linoleum surrounding the toilets starting to dissolve where people had missed the bowls and not cleaned up after themselves. Piles of laundry had been left all over the living room floor and cleaning all that up kept me occupied for another afternoon.

It was a beautiful house, with gorgeous open verandahs looking onto stunning views of the rain forest on the nearby hillsides, but it was in the tropics and was horribly humid. There were no insect screens, air conditioning or overhead fans, and the only way to keep it cool was to leave all the doors and windows open.

This meant the house was crawling with insects. There were stick insects, spiders, flies, ants, moths, beetles, mosquitoes, cockroaches and God knows what else. The place was full of cobwebs and insect nests. I had a standing fan in my bedroom which kept the mosquitoes off during the night, but for the rest of the time, I was a living target. Despite smothering myself in insect repellent, I was eaten alive. I was just hoping I didn't get Ross River Fever (something one of the local residents had caught and had ended up in a wheelchair from).

When I first saw all the cobwebs and insect nests, I thought one of the first things I'd do would be to remove them, but again I couldn't face it, so I just tried to avoid the worst areas.

The worst time was at night, when the house lights would attract all sorts of moths and flying insects. I'd lie in bed in the darkness and suddenly there'd be a thump on the pillow beside me as some creepy crawly fell out of the air. I'd pin the sheet down around my head and practically suffocate, trying to avoid coming into contact with them.

The owner's son was supposed to be moving out when they left for their holiday, but he was still there on the Monday after they'd gone. Then, on the Tuesday, he went missing, as did the dog. I searched the pub and his grandmother's, but no one had seen him.

The next day, when I got home, the dog had reappeared and a few items had been moved around, so I presumed the son had returned the dog and gone to his new residence. However, a week later he was still coming and going without ever telling me when he'd be around, which I found rather disconcerting. At one point he came in and went to his room.

An hour later, when Steve called me on Skype and asked how it was going with the son, I didn't know if he was in the house or not and told Steve how weird I was finding the situation.

Next day the son announced his arrival and started packing up a bag of clothes. He didn't return after that, so I presume he must have overheard my conversation and decided it was time to go.

WATER DAMAGE

In between keeping house, walking the dog, petting the cat and helping out at the spa, I was glued to the television. The floodwaters had worked their way south and were about to hit Brisbane. The news provided extended bulletins every night, with reports of the latest towns to be affected.

By Wednesday 12 January 2011, Brisbane was inundated. The central business district was shut down and people were being moved to evacuation centres around the periphery. The Wivenhoe dam was in danger of breaching its walls, so huge amounts of water had to be released to relieve the pressure. This wave of released water caused what was being described as an "inland tsunami", which devastated a small town downstream of it.

The news was full of stories of communities being destroyed. I received tonnes of emails from people back home, wanting to know if I'd been affected and I was relieved to be able to report that I'd managed to avoid getting caught in any of the major trouble spots.

CAIRNS REVISITED

On one of my first days off, I decided to go to Cairns to visit my old stomping ground from when I'd lived there in 1989. The owner had left me her car, which was making getting around a lot easier (and cooler), so it seemed like a good opportunity to make the trip without being weighed down by my bike clothes.

I had been so looking forward to going back to Cairns – but oh my God, what a mess they'd made of it. Obviously the property developers had got hold of the place and were more interested in increasing their bank balances than in preserving the essence of the town. Every spare bit of land had been filled with either a horrible hotel or a hideous shopping centre. What used to be a lovely, open, low-level town with a sense of space and plenty of green areas had been transformed into a concrete labyrinth. And, worst of all, the lovely little house we used to live in and that I had such happy memories of had been knocked down and replaced by a set of soulless apartment blocks.

On the plus side, the central plaza was still pretty much the same and the Esplanade had been very nicely landscaped to include a swimming area, but beyond that I wasn't impressed.

I stopped off at Kuranda (a 1960s market town) on the way home. This, I'm pleased to report, was still exactly the same as it had been since the beginning of time, so all was not lost.

NAKED RIDING

After a few days of air conditioned luxury in the car, I decided it was time to take the bike for a spin again, so I rode it down to the spa and back. This was the first time I'd ridden it naked (that is to say, unladen) for weeks, and what a difference it made.

The road to the coast crosses the Great Dividing Range and is another twisty one, full of hairpin bends and steep descents, but I managed it with scarcely a touch on the brakes. It reminded me of how much I used to love riding – back in the days before I lost my confidence and became a gibbering wreck. Not that I'd been that bad for quite some time, but it was great being able to throw the bike around a bit for a change and not worry about it all collapsing beneath me.

I must make special mention of the unsung hero of my travels here. The bike, which was a stallion of a machine, was a magnificent travelling companion. It had stayed upright despite having the most nervous of riders at its reins and it had provided utterly reliable service day after day in the most challenging conditions. It even had great fuel economy, despite the mass of luggage it had to bear. I couldn't have asked for a more trusted steed and I felt very lucky to have found it.

I was looking forward to getting out on it some more, without all the baggage, and really letting it run free. Do I sound like I'm talking about a horse here? Well, I guess a motorbike is something of a mechanical horse, albeit not so frisky.

THE WET

About a week into my stay and the wet season was well and truly upon us. One day I took the dog for a walk to have a look at a lovely old Queenslander-style house that was for sale on a nearby hill. Just as we got there, the heavens opened, and we had to shelter on the verandah for about half an hour while the rain subsided enough for us to run home. And it pretty much continued raining from that point on.

The rain brought out a huge plague of "flying ants", which swarmed the kitchen. These looked like petals being blown in the wind, but they were actually termites that lose their wings and burrow into the woodwork of your house. Hundreds of small, leaf-like wings were left all over my nice clean kitchen.

The rains also heralded the first appearance of bats in the house. All this, combined with the presence of frogs, geckos (small lizards) and all the other insects that were regular boarders, not to mention the dog having several barking fits during the night, left me feeling somewhat shaken. By the end of the second week, I had practically decided I should move out and entrust the care of the house and pets to the owner's son. I even got as far as writing an email to that effect, but my internet account ran out of credit and I couldn't log on to send it.

By the next morning, I had re-assessed the situation and decided I needed to focus on all the positive aspects of living in the house. Within a few hours I started to feel better and, after a particularly fun evening in the pub, I had changed my mind and decided to stay. After all, what kind of adventurer would I be if I ran away after only two weeks because of a houseful of squirming creepy crawlies?

FREAKING OUT

As if to test me, a praying mantis flew into the living room the next night. The cat immediately went after it and half-killed it, but left it with just enough life to flounder on the floor for a few hours (I couldn't bring myself to put it out of its misery). So, after another sleepless night with the dog barking at every shadow that passed by, my resolve for staying in the house was severely dented. That afternoon, I came home to find the writhing dissected innards of a cockroach on the kitchen floor, with the cat looking on, a gecko in her mouth and a crazed look on her face.

So, in answer to my previous question, it would appear I'm the type of adventurer that has absolutely no stomach for insects. To say they were *creeping me out* would be the understatement of the year. I couldn't stand them!!! By the end of the day I was seriously thinking I would have to look into finding some alternative accommodation with fly screens and air cooling devices, because this was freaking me out.

The next day, the cat had disappeared so I went in search of her. Until this point I had avoided going into the son's room, but as this was the only place I hadn't looked, I ventured in. I was greeted by a foul, but slightly familiar odour. As I peered around, I saw a large plastic bucket sitting next to the bed, half-filled with a strange yellow fluid.

Suddenly I put two and two together. Oh my God, the son had a piss-pot in his room! Revolted, I fled and threw myself in the shower. The very thought of being in the same space as such an offensive item made me want to vomit, and the sooner I got any trace of it off my skin the better. Could this get any worse?

Working at the spa was also making me feel increasingly uncomfortable. When a lady came in, asked me how I came to be working there and revealed that she worked for the government (albeit not the Immigration Service), I decided it was time to leave. Although strictly speaking I was allowed to do voluntary work, I didn't want to find myself in a situation where my work status could be questioned. Besides, it was actually costing me money to work there, as I had to pay for all my petrol costs, which were starting to mount up.

FITTING IN

Ever since arriving in Mount Molloy, I'd felt slightly out of place. Although the owner of the house had introduced me to most of her family and many of the local residents, I didn't really feel I fitted in. The owner's sister was very kind and supportive and took me to the pub every Friday night, as this was when all the locals got together, but I didn't feel I had that much in common with them.

It was the same with the people at the spa. There was a lovely woman there of about my age who I really liked, but apart from her, I didn't feel I connected with any of the other staff.

As a result I found, for the first time since arriving in Australia, that I felt quite alone in Mount Molloy. Although I'd been travelling by myself for several months by now, this was the first time I'd really felt this way. Everywhere else I'd gone, I seemed to meet people I connected with at the drop of a hat, but Mount Molloy was different.

There was no one I could share my mounting unease with, and when I can't vent how I'm feeling, I get very tense and things that usually wouldn't bother me take on a much more overwhelming feel. This was my state of mind when I got more news from home.

HOMEWARD BOUND

That weekend, I spoke to my mum and also my dad, whose health issues weren't improving. It turned out my dad was having difficulty walking (a fact I hadn't previously appreciated) and that my mum was very stressed because my step-father's condition was deteriorating.

By the end of these conversations, I had an overwhelming desire to go back and help them. That night I agonised about what I should do. On the one hand, I'd made a commitment to be in Mount Molloy for three months, but on the other hand, my parents needed my help. Plus, all the creepy crawlies, the starlight barking of the dog, the working at the spa and the growing sense of isolation meant the reasons for leaving were starting to far outweigh those for staying. But I hate walking away from a promise and if it hadn't been for the fact that I knew the owner's son was still around and would be able to look after the pets, I probably would have stayed. By the next morning I'd made my decision.

I phoned the owner's sister to get a contact address for the owner. "Is everything all right?" she asked. As I replied, I burst into tears.

"I'm going to have to go home," I bubbled.

She was great, though. She took the situation in hand and arranged for the son to move back in and take care of the pets, and to contact the owner to let her know. We agreed I'd leave on the Thursday, after which I'd start making my way back to Melbourne (as this was where my flight would depart from).

Having just done a massive ride up to Mount Molloy, I decided to allow myself a bit more time to get back again. I aimed to be back in Melbourne by the end of February and home by early March. As the east coast was still affected by the floods, I thought I'd go inland and return via the "red centre" (Ayres Rock and Alice Springs). I might then try and "nip" across to Canberra and Bateman's Bay, to catch up with friends before returning to Melbourne.

My trip was originally meant to be for a year, but as I'd done pretty much all the things I went to Australia to do (apart from crossing the Nullarbor) and had had more adventure than most people have in their lives, I felt that returning home after seven months was still a pretty good result.

BACK ON THE ROAD

So, exactly three weeks after I'd arrived, I was back on the road again. I left Mount Molloy on Thursday 27 January 2011 and rode the 100-odd km down to Cairns. I felt as though I'd been released from prison. Staying in an insect-free room at the YHA in Cairns made me acutely aware of how much anxiety I'd been carrying in my body since arriving in Mount Molloy and I luxuriated in the comfort of a screen protected, air conditioned room.

Before I left, I ordered a new set of panniers for the bike, because one of the old ones had developed a large tear. This meant I needed to stay in Cairns for a few days until they arrived. It felt good to be back this time; even though it wasn't the town it used to be, enough of it was still the same to make me feel at home.

I felt bad about leaving Mount Molloy before I was supposed to. I liked to think of myself as a dependable person, but all the insects and the needs of my parents made me realise it was time to go. I'd made sure there was enough food for the pets and someone to look after them, but I still felt bad that I was letting the owners down.

However, I felt let down by them, too. The house was a mess, the situation with the son was very unsettling and I'd felt pressured into working at the spa. The relief I felt at leaving proved to me that I had made the right decision.

Chapter 13: Racing Hurricanes

CHANGE OF HEART

Contrary to my first thoughts, I decided to return to Melbourne via the east coast, as going through the red centre at this time of year would mean dealing with temperatures in excess of 45°C and I wasn't sure I was up to that again. The east coast route, in contrast, would only be a mere 30°C. Plus, it was a much more populated and interesting route and was also a more direct line to Canberra and Bateman's Bay, where my friends were.

The only trouble was, there were two cyclones (or hurricanes, as we call them in Britain) developing off shore, so there might be more high winds and flooding to contend with. But either way, there would be risks involved, and I felt I'd rather take my chances on the coast than bake in the desert again.

My plan was to spend two weeks getting from Cairns to Noosa (just north of Brisbane), where I could stay with a friend of my brother's. After that, I'd take another two weeks from Noosa to Canberra, followed by a final week or so getting back round to Melbourne. I'd stay there for a week so that I could sell the bike before flying to Hong Kong, where my brother lived, on about 12 March and back to the UK a few days later. Along the way, I hoped to take in places like the Whitsundays, Fraser Island, Byron Bay, Coff's Harbour, Newcastle and Palm Beach (aka "Summer Bay") where they film the Aussie soap opera *Home and Away*). So it was going to be a great trip and I intended to savour every moment.

I felt quite sad that my adventure was coming to an end. I'd had the most wonderful time and was overjoyed that I'd actually managed to ride the width of Australia in nine days. It would have been great to have had some romance, but the lack of it gave me the opportunity to really focus on the wondrous scenery around me and fully appreciate every moment of the fantastic adventure I was having. Despite all the fear of riding a bike that was way too heavy for me, travelling through Australia's varied terrains had been a fabulous experience and I loved watching it all pass by. I loved being in such close contact with nature and I felt strangely at home in the vast, empty expanses of the outback. Something about the isolation forced me to come out of my shell and connect with people again.

Maybe it's because everyone is so much more vulnerable in that type of environment that people are more willing to help each other, but I found I was extremely happy there. As for romance – well who knew? I still had six weeks to go . . .

POOLSIDE

Whilst in Cairns I decided to do a bit of sunbathing, so I donned my bikini and headed down to the lagoon on the Esplanade. This was the first time I'd done any sunbathing since I'd arrived in Australia and, like most Brits abroad, my stunning white flesh practically blinded the locals. I did, of course, use sunscreen, but when I later got changed I realised I hadn't applied it very evenly, as my tummy and legs were covered in red blotches where I'd obviously missed some bits.

One thing I'm happy to report about Australia is that the men there still uphold the fine tradition of short shorts and what the locals call "budgie smugglers" (i.e. Speedo-style swimming trunks). I quite enjoyed observing the extra bit of flesh that was on display around me.

ROUND THE BEND

I got the call late that afternoon saying my new panniers had arrived, so the following morning I jumped on the bike and headed up to Atherton to collect them. (I'd ordered them from the same place I'd got my tyres from, as I thought I'd be going back that way before I changed my mind and decided to go down the coast instead.)

I took the road to Mareeba via Kuranda, which was very twisty, and joined the Kennedy Highway to Atherton. I collected the panniers and then took the road over the Gillies Ranges down to Gordonville. Now I've done some winding roads since being in Australia, but this one took the biscuit. About 30 km of hairpin bends and steep descents, with amazing views over the Great Dividing Range it was fantastic.

CALM BEFORE THE STORM

When I left Mount Molloy, the owner's brother-in-law told me to watch out for two cyclones making their way towards the coast. However, I was too busy trying to fit the plastic supports inside my new panniers so they wouldn't collapse again (I think this was why the last set ripped) to pay much attention to the weather reports. I was up at the crack of dawn on Sunday 30 January and on my way south. I wasn't exactly sure how far I'd go, but Townsville seemed like a good target.

As I rode into a petrol station on the way out of Cairns, I was surprised to notice that I rode over the gutter and right up to the pump without a second thought. I'd developed a bad habit of stopping about a metre away from petrol pumps and paddling the bike in, just in case I lost control and ploughed into one of them. Could it be that I was finally getting used to all my luggage?

Leaving the petrol station behind and joining the highway, I noticed something else about my ridiculous amount of baggage. At first it seemed like a real burden, but now I was feeling quite comfortable with it and even quite liked it. I guess I'd been carrying a lot of emotional baggage around with me for a long time, but during the course of the trip I'd started to let go of it. But there were still some things I was clinging on to – somewhat like my excess baggage.

People often asked me, "Have you never thought about getting rid of some of it?", to which I'd reply, "There's nothing I can get rid of." And I guess it was the same for me emotionally: there were certain aspects of my personality I couldn't get rid of. So, over time, I'd gradually started to accept them. I may not have been at the point of "liking" them all yet, but I was certainly more comfortable with them.

It was a fantastic ride south on the Bruce Highway. Somehow all my nerves had gone and I was loving every moment. I'd been down this road many times before but I still adored it. It's sugar cane country between Cairns and Tully, then banana country from Tully to Ingham.

Everything was so green and lush and the Great Dividing Range to the right provided a spectacular backdrop.

I meandered my way along, stopping at various places like Tully and Mission Beach. On the way down to Mission Beach there were lots of signs warning motorists to drive slowly to avoid colliding with cassowaries. Cassowaries are big, emu-like birds with long, dark, straw-like plumage, midnight-blue heads and a red collar and wattle. They are only found in a few places in Australia, so their protection is important.

Some of the signs say "Cassowaries seen here recently" and, as I was wondering just how recent "recently" was, I suddenly spotted one. As it's very rare to see them, I screeched to a halt, jumped off the bike, grabbed my camera and set off in hot pursuit. And there it was in the undergrowth, foraging around. What luck!

Mission Beach was the same as it had been six years earlier when I was last there, albeit not as sunny. Tully was similar, but it was good to see these places again and be reminded of all the fun Lisa and I had had, learning how to be White Water River Guides back in '89.

By about 1 pm, I had reached Townsville. I'd already done 400-odd km, so I decided to stop there for the night. As there wasn't a youth hostel in Townsville anymore, I thought I should camp (after all, I'd been carrying all this camping gear for thousands of miles so I felt I really ought to use it). I made my way to the caravan site on the foreshore and asked for a tent site. The lady behind the desk responded, "You do know there's a cyclone coming in tonight, don't you?"

"Er, vaguely," I replied, having pretty much forgotten about it.

She showed me a weather chart with the cyclone heading straight for Mackay, the next big town south. Not realising Mackay was actually about 250 km away, I let myself be persuaded to take a cabin instead of a tent site, for five times the cost. This left me feeling somewhat stung, especially seeing as I wasn't convinced that the cabin would survive the storm any better than a tent.

The lady at the desk suggested I park the bike in the concrete toilet block overnight, so that it wouldn't get blown across the park if the cyclone hit.

That night, I could see a huge grey storm front building out to sea and making its way towards us. Thinking this was the cyclone, I stashed the bike in the loos as instructed, battened down the hatches and made sure everything in my cabin was on the floor before the hurricane hit us.

ANTHONY AND THE GOLIATH

I awoke to a calm and peaceful morning. Cyclone Anthony, the first of the two cyclones, had hit Bowen, a town about 150 km south, but we were unaffected in Townsville.

By the time I'd retrieved my bike from the toilets (which I did in my shorts and T-shirt and was surprised at how free I felt), it was about 7 am before I got on the road. Nevertheless I made good time, got to Ayr by 8.30 and stopped for a cuppa in the local servo.

The headline on the newspaper read "Anthony and the Goliath" and had a picture of a massive cyclone building out to sea. The girl behind the desk was quick to advise me that I'd be best to head as far inland as possible and get away from the coast because this second cyclone (Cyclone

Yasi, aka Goliath), currently over Fiji, would be a Category 4 and would destroy everything in its path.

As I'd already missed the turn-off for the Flinders Highway west, I left the servo like a bat out of hell and continued south, with the intention of turning off at Mackay. However, by the time I reached Bowen, where Anthony had struck, and got the chance to consider the girl's advice, I decided I'd be better off getting as far south as possible. Cyclone Yasi wasn't due to hit until Thursday, which gave me another two days to clear the strike zone.

The Bruce Highway skims the western edge of Bowen which appeared to have escaped harm. I stopped in a service station for lunch and the locals told me there had been a fair amount of damage to the main town, but I didn't have time to stop and investigate. Two days wasn't that much time to cover the remaining 800–900 km to Noosa, where I'd be safe. So much for spending a month meandering my way down the coast – at this rate, I was going to be in Sydney by the weekend.

I made Mackay by 1 pm. I then ran into a strange phenomenon that I hadn't encountered in Australia before – a traffic jam. A van had run into the side of a bridge, which meant that all the traffic from four different directions was backed up for miles. It took me two hours to travel the 30 km from Mackay to the next town, Sarina.

I stopped for the night in a small village called Carmila, about 100 km south of Mackay. Unlike most of the towns on this route, which were bisected by the Bruce Highway, you had to turn off the highway into this one. After a short ride down the wide main street I crossed a railway track, saw the hotel on the right and pulled up.

It was quite an old hotel, with a bit of a frog problem in the showers, but the people were very friendly and helpful and let me park my bike round the back out of sight. I settled in for another peaceful, air conditioned night. I was hoping to make it to Hervey Bay the next day.

DODGING DISASTER

Having fled south like a Wild West outlaw for the last three days, I saw a newspaper report the next morning which almost made me weep. It said Cyclone Yasi was now heading for Rockhampton, a town about 200 km south from my current position and exactly where I was heading.

The thought of riding all that way and still getting caught in it was almost more than I could bear. However, I knew I still had a day to get clear of the area, so I decided just to batter on south.

I left Carmila at 6.15 am and whacked off the first 128 km to Marlborough by 7.30. One serving of bacon and eggs and two cups of tea later, I was back on the road and in Rockhampton by 9.30. Then it all started going pear-shaped. Rockhampton was one of the towns worst affected by the floods and although there wasn't a lot of evidence of it in the town itself (either they'd done a spectacular clean-up job or my route didn't go past the worst areas), there were countless roadworks southwards, where they were piecing the road back together again, so progress became quite slow.

As a result, I didn't make it to Hervey Bay that day. Instead, I stopped at a small town called Gin Gin, which seemed to be a major truck stop with road trains parked on every piece of spare verge. I'd seen a sign for a motel called *The Flying Scotsman,* so I figured that would be the one for me. Unfortunately, it turned out to be way out of my budget, so I swung round and went back up the main street to another, less luxurious one.

After my experience in Cunnamulla, I'd taken to asking to see the room before committing to it. When I made my request at this motel, the lady rather tersely replied, "What d'you want to see it for? It's got a bed, a TV, air conditioning – what more do you want?"

I was tempted to say, "Well, there can be a vast difference in the quality of the decor and furnishings," but I realised this would probably inflame her further, so I took it without further argument.

It actually turned out to be fine. I had a quick swim in the pool and then went across to one of the many roadhouses for dinner. The news was reporting that Cyclone Yasi was now heading towards Cairns, so it appeared I'd managed to outrun the most imminent danger. Thank goodness. I wasn't sure I could have kept up that pace for much longer – I'd been doing 400–500 km a day. Interestingly enough, though, this kind of distance was now becoming quite manageable for me.

IN-FLIGHT ENTERTAINMENT

Most of the time, I was quite happy riding along by myself, but that day I could really have done with some companionship. Mile after mile of endless bush and only my thoughts to keep me company.

You may wonder what I thought about while I was beetling along. Well, for a long time I'd had the constant commentary of the anonymous voice in my head, criticising every move I made, but now I seemed to be a lot more at peace. If I wasn't thinking about what to write in my next blog entry, the main thing I seemed to do was read road signs – you know, "Road Work Ahead, Reduce Speed", "Overtaking Lane 300 m Ahead" or "What is the highest mountain in Queensland?"

Yes, that was one of the signs. Because it's such a boring stretch of road, the authorities suggest you should play "trivia games" to stop yourself from nodding off and this is a question they give you to get you started. All very well, if you've got someone to play it with. (The answer, by the way, is Mount Bartley Frere.)

MOOD SWINGS

The next day, the ride from Gin Gin to Noosa Heads found me in a rotten mood. I was hot, tired and fed up with riding alone with no one to talk to. Everywhere I'd gone in Australia, I'd met people and always had the chance to pass the time of day, if not hang out with people. But I seemed to have drifted out of the flow, and apart from motel and petrol station owners, had barely spoken to another soul since leaving Cairns.

The scenery had become quite boring too. After Mackay, the farmlands and seaside towns had petered out and it had become mile after mile of featureless bush. And more roadworks – at one point I got so hot waiting in a long queue of traffic that I pulled the bike over to the side, got my bottle of water out and started pouring it all over myself. It was only when I'd finished that I noticed the truck driver behind me, sitting with a big smile on his face watching the whole affair.

As I got closer to Noosa it became more built up, with a corresponding increase in traffic. I was hot and irritable and as I turned off the main highway I was confronted with a series of roundabouts funnelling me towards the town centre. On a previous visit I'd got lost in these roundabouts and ended up being spat back out and missing the town altogether, but on this occasion, despite my bad temper, I managed to ride right up to the door of the YHA without a single wrong turn.

Another small, stuffy room with no air conditioning. I was not a happy bunny.

DEVASTATION

That evening, the news was full of reports of the impending impact of Cyclone Yasi. It was now off the coast of Cairns and, as it was due to make landfall that night, all towns between Cairns and Rockhampton had been evacuated (part of the reason the roads had been so quiet).

During the night, Yasi finally hit Queensland. Mission Beach and Tully (the places I'd stopped at a few days before) took the brunt of it and were almost completely destroyed. It was reported that not a single building in either of these towns had escaped being damaged in some way. Luckily the evacuation procedures had ensured that no one was seriously injured. Queensland had again suffered a massive blow, but its people were still standing.

FAMILY FRIENDSHIPS

I managed to make contact with my brother's friend Andrew, and the next day he came and took me off to the comfort of their gorgeous country home, complete with swimming pool, fans and air conditioning.

Andrew was my brother's best friend at school and although I hadn't seen him much since then, it was lovely to meet him again. I'd been starved of human company over the last few days and the stress of trying to outrun the cyclone meant I was in need of some serious TLC.

Andrew took me for a delicious lunch at a local café and we spent the afternoon chatting about all the things that had happened to us since we were kids. I was astonished to learn that he'd now been out in Australia for over twenty-five years and his children had been born and grown up there. Was it really that long since he used to come round to our house to see Chris?

Andrew had always been a bit of a boffin and now had his own IT consultancy firm. He'd obviously done very well for himself, as he'd managed to fulfil the great Aussie dream and had built his own house. In the evening, his wife Linda and their two children made a gorgeous seafood dinner for us. I really liked Linda; she was a typical Australian with a fun sense of humour and strong views on everything, and we chatted into the night.

I had a great visit with Andrew and his family and, when I left the following morning, I found myself biting back the tears again. It was so good to be with people I knew and to be looked after. I'd been alone for too long and the sudden reconnection and disconnection made me very emotional.

I left Andrew's about 9.30 am, which ensured that I missed the rush hour traffic into Brisbane but meant I ended up doing most of the 300 km to Byron Bay in the sweltering heat of the day. It seemed to take me longer to cover distances when it was really hot and it was 4 pm before I got there. Unfortunately, the YHA was fully booked, so I found a campsite which had small "lodges" available (all the tent sites were taken) and booked into one of these for three nights. I'd been on the road for almost a week and felt exhausted, so I needed to recharge.

FUN IN THE SUN

Byron Bay was just what I needed – rest and relaxation in beautiful surroundings. The campsite was right on the beach and therefore benefitted from cool sea breezes as well as warm sunshine. It was a bit of a hippy town – lots of massage clinics, art galleries and shops selling brightly coloured clothing and weird-smelling things. And more campervans than I'd seen in my entire tour of Australia – it was a big surfing destination.

I was there over a weekend and on the Friday night a group of twenty-something lads, followed by a separate group of twenty-something girls, checked into the two lodges next to mine. Not surprisingly, the two groups instantly bonded, the music was cranked up and the booze began to flow. Bless them, though, they very kindly asked if I would like to join them, so I had a cocktail and then politely left them to it. It's just as well I'm pretty deaf, as I managed to sleep through the ensuing din.

Saturday was spent cleaning the bike, wandering around acquainting myself with the town and walking up and down the beach in my bikini in an attempt to get a tan. I mention this only because, in a town full of twenty-year-old stick insects, one does become particularly conscious of one's "fuller figure". Anyway, I managed to get a bit of a tan and more burns on the areas that I missed again with the sunscreen.

Sunday I went sea kayaking. This was brilliant fun and, as they didn't have enough canoes for everyone, I got paired up with one of the guides, Shane, a very attractive man from New Zealand. Shane encouraged us all to stand up and see if we could see some dolphins from an "aerial perspective", which resulted in me nose-diving into the sea. Later, a shoal of fish was having a feeding frenzy on the surface but no dolphins were to be seen. Shane leant over and said, "Just between you and me, it probably means there are sharks about."

Jesus Christ, I thought – *thank God he didn't tell me that before I had my little dip.*

On the way back, a lady got a bit panicky, so Shane offered to take her back in to shore. This meant I had to get onto her kayak. I managed not to plunge into the water this time, but I ended up on my back with my legs split between the two drifting canoes before I finally managed to pull myself aboard – not the most elegant manoeuvre.

Later that day I had an aura photograph taken. It was really interesting. They sit you in a seat that resembles an executioner's chair and you have to put your hands on electrodes at either side. They then take a picture of you with a special camera. A few minutes later, you get a Polaroid photo of yourself enshrouded in colour. I had a mostly green aura, which meant I was going through a massive "healing" process. I then had to choose a small stone from a basket, and I chose one which represented "manifestation". So I was healing from past wounds and entering a period of manifestation. This felt good and left me feeling quite hopeful about my future.

I was having such a nice time in Byron Bay that I decided to stay another day. However, the weather changed and became quite wet and windy, so I did a pile of laundry in the morning and then took a walk up to the lighthouse. Oh, it was so nice to feel the cool wind and rain on my skin after so many days of sweltering heat.

Four days of fun in the sun and it was time to move on again. Byron's Bay had been just the tonic I needed after my race to outrun the hurricanes. Feeling revived, I packed up the bike and hit the road again.

Chapter 14: Men

COLD CHILLS AND HOT FLUSHES

I'd had high hopes about experiencing some romance during my return ride to Melbourne, but so far I'd hardly met another soul, let alone a potential love interest. But things were about to change.

I left Byron Bay on a cold, drizzly morning. In fact, it got so cold at one point, I had to pull over and dig out my windproof inner jacket. However, by the time I arrived in Port Macquarie it had brightened up and I was able to have a very pleasant stroll around the town. There was a youth hostel there so I checked in.

The next morning I woke up with huge bites on both my lower legs. I'd made the mistake of sleeping with my legs outside the sheet and had obviously been ravished by some mysterious flesh-eating beasties during the night. Even after applying copious amounts of sting reliever, the itching was almost unbearable.

It was quite cool again that day but it brightened up later and by the time I got to Newcastle it was delightful. Instead of joining the Newcastle/Sydney Freeway, I decided to follow the Pacific Highway into the town, which took me all round the coastal beaches of Newcastle and beyond. It was really pretty, with lots of lidos and Victorian-style changing rooms and shelters.

When I was in Townsville, awaiting the arrival of the first hurricane, I'd managed to make contact with Glenn and John, the knights in black leather who had rescued me at the Wilcannia service station and escorted me across the desert to Cobar. As they were based in the Northern Beaches area of Sydney, I asked them if they might be interested in guiding me to nearby Palm Beach. Glenn gladly agreed and told me to phone him when I arrived. He also made some comment along the lines, "Don't worry, we'll introduce you to plenty of, erm, people."

After leaving Newcastle, the road made its way down a narrow peninsula, surrounded by sea on one side and lakes on the other. It was beautiful riding, but eventually I had to join the freeway into Sydney. Having spent the better part of the last two weeks on fairly deserted roads, rejoining the busy freeway system was a bit of a shock to the system and instantly brought my nerves back.

But thanks to some excellent directions from John, I managed to make it to the YHA at the Northern Beaches without a single wrong turn. I then made contact with Glenn, who invited me round for dinner. I had a lovely evening with Glenn, his wife Emilia, John and their other friends, Mark and Stephan.

It was only when Emilia announced, "Jill, all these men are single and don't get a good meal very often," that I realised I'd been set up. Glenn must have read the bit in my blog about wishing I'd had some romance and thought he could help out in this department. This must have been what he'd meant by his previous comment.

I was mortified. I could feel my face flush scarlet and could barely even look at John after that, let alone make conversation (after all, he was a very good-looking man).

If left to my own devices when meeting men I'm generally quite relaxed and comfortable with them, but when someone publicly announces an expression of interest (either mine or theirs), I find myself cringing with embarrassment. This stems from when I was at school and, every time I fancied a guy, my best friend at the time would announce this to his face, which invariably resulted in streams of laughter and me going bright red. Try as I might, it was a reaction I just couldn't throw off.

NORTHERN BEACHES SOCIAL RIDERS

Glenn and Emilia invited me to come and stay at their house, so the next day I left the YHA and moved in with them. Glenn had a pest control business so, suspecting I'd been bitten by bed bugs at the YHA in Port Macquarie and not wanting to contaminate their bed with them, I asked him what he thought my bites were from. They had now merged into one giant red rash on each leg, which made it look as if I'd burnt them on my exhausts. He assured me they were just mosquito bites, but it didn't stop them itching.

Glenn and Emilia were a great couple and I spent the next three days with them and the Northern Beaches Social Riders. This was the motorcycle club that Glenn ran but it wasn't just any old motorcycle club; they also raised money for children's charities, tonnes of it – so far they had raised over $300,000. They did this through a combination of raffles, events and people paying to be pillion passengers on their rides.

Thursday night was raffle night at the pub and then on the Friday night they had a big ride through the streets of Sydney. The main instruction I was given was, "Ride in staggered formation and keep as close as possible to the person in front so that no cars can break up the group."

Easier said than done, I have to say. Bearing in mind that most of the riding I'd been doing over the last six months had been in pretty remote areas where you could go for miles before you saw another vehicle, having to ride at a distance of approximately ten feet from the bike in front came as something of a challenge to me. Add to that the fact that I had absolutely no idea where we were going and was surrounded by enormous Harley-Davidsons, and you have all the makings of some absolutely appalling riding from yours truly.

Initially we passed through some suburban areas, but after a while we joined the motorway system. It was getting dark and everyone sped off at breakneck speed. I had to ride way faster than I normally would to keep up with them and, as this was the first time I wasn't wearing my protective trousers, I kept having visions of parting company with my bike and becoming a big mangled mess on the tarmac.

Cars were coming at us from all directions and, contrary to instructions, I was letting them in, so I then had to apply even more speed to overtake them and rejoin the group. My heart was thumping.

The marshals did a spectacular job of riding up in front of the joining traffic, sitting in front of it with their hand held up in a "stop" gesture until the group had passed, and then bombing past us all again to take up their positions at the front of the group.

Arriving at Harry's Pie Shop at Woollamolloo (a local Sydney institution), I was, once again, a gibbering wreck. Pouring out my terror to anyone who would listen seemed to clear my nerves a bit and on the way back I got it together and did a much better job of keeping tight with the pack and actually found I was really enjoying myself.

The return route went right through the centre of downtown Sydney, past all the late-night shoppers, who stopped in their tracks to take in the noise and spectacle of thirty Harley-Davidsons (and one Suzuki) making their way past. I knew where we were now, as we stopped and started our way up Sydney's main drag. My engine was roasting as I kept accelerating forward and then braking to stop. We went up past the bars in Kings Cross, past the railway station and the Central YHA where I'd stayed on my last visit, and then I was lost again.

I had no idea where we were or even which direction we were going in. I figured we must be going north in order to get back to where we'd started from, but this was logic talking, as my sense of orientation had been left behind at Harry's Pie Shop.

Glenn and Emilia, John and the rest of the NBSR were a fabulous group of people and my heartfelt thanks went out to everyone who chatted to me and made me feel so welcome. I felt especially grateful to Glenn and Emilia, who welcomed me into their home, barely knowing me, and showed me some of the local sights.

While I was there, I also got a chance to take a ride out to *Home and Away's* "Summer Bay", and saw a few of the key landmarks used in the series. There was a film crew there but alas, I couldn't spot any of the cast.

On the Saturday I moved back to the Northern Beaches YHA, as Glenn and Emilia were going away. I was feeling a mixture of deep gratitude and nervous exhaustion. Although it was lovely meeting everyone at the NBSR, I've always found encountering lots of new people quite nerve-wracking, so I was looking forward to being able to spend a bit of time alone again. This seemed strange given only a week before I'd been desperate for company, but this had almost been too much company. I needed to find a balance between too many people and not enough.

I decided to stay at the YHA for a few days and then make my way down to Bateman's Bay, where I'd see my old friend, Rod.

TIME TRAVELLING

After a day or so of wandering about the Northern Beaches, I took the bus into central Sydney. It was about six and a half years since I'd been there last, but as I looked out across Circular Quay (which, incidentally, is rectangular), it seemed like only yesterday. It's funny how memories can distort time – or is it how time can distort memories? As I travelled down the east coast I went through lots of places I'd been through before, yet didn't recognise at all. Then there were others that I had really clear memories of in my head, but didn't even see this time. Weird, isn't it?

I took a tour of the Sydney Opera House. Wow – it's impressive from the outside, but inside, it really takes your breath away. The "sails" that form the roof rise up from the floor in cathedral-like arches, creating a cavernous space below them. Regrettably, they wouldn't let us take any pictures of the inside, so I had to add those images to the reliable stack of memories in my head.

STRANGEWAYS

The first time I went to Sydney, back in 1989, I hated it. I was staying in King's Cross, which, as well as having lots of backpackers' hostels, is the red light district. I'd left my friends in Cairns and come down to the big city to make some money doing temp work, but I felt very alone and threatened in that area and went back to Cairns after two weeks.

When I went back to Sydney in 2004, though, I had a completely different experience. This time I stayed in the Central YHA by the train station and, during an outing to Bondi Beach, met a gorgeous guy called Tony in a coffee shop, who later took me out for the evening. We had a wonderful time, ending in a brief romantic encounter which left me swooning for weeks. So I re-assessed my view of the city and, with the aid of my now rose-coloured spectacles, found I really liked it.

However, staying at the Northern Beaches YHA made me uneasy again. It was quite shabby and few people seemed to observe the YHA rule about cleaning up after themselves. Most of the people there seemed to be long-term travellers who were working in Sydney, but there were also some rather strange people staying there.

First, there was the 68-year-old lady who'd just broken up with her boyfriend in the hope that it would force him to change certain aspects of his behaviour and she'd then be able to get back together with him. It made me wonder if we ever really grow up and stop playing games with people. There was also the thirty-something girl who kept going out on "dates" with various men, not returning until the wee small hours and sleeping all day. And the woman who'd play about on her laptop all night long. Then there was the other biker.

He'd arrived at some point and parked his bike next to mine in the car park. The day before I was due to leave Sydney, I was down at my bike, tinkering about, when he came out and began working on his. We started talking; he told me about his trip and I told him about mine. When I mentioned I'd been out in the outback, he asked me lots of questions about how I found the people in Queensland. I told him I'd met some wonderful folk and was really impressed by how helpful they had been.

He seemed really surprised about this and started talking about all the horror stories that had happened to various travellers over the years. He seemed a little too interested in these, so I decided to make myself scarce.

When I was leaving the next day and started my bike up, it gave the most enormous back-fire and then, when I pulled off, it felt like the tyres had been let down.

As I'd left the other biker still working on his bike the day before, I wondered if he'd sabotaged mine, just to prove his point that not all Australians are lovely people. However, when I got to the petrol station and checked my tyre pressures, they were only a couple of PSI under what they should be and I started to think I was getting a bit paranoid. Just as well I was leaving.

ROUTE NO 3

I left Sydney on Wednesday 16 February 2011. The thought of riding through the biggest city in Australia on a fully laden motorbike wasn't one that I'd been particularly looking forward to, but I noticed that Route No 3 from Mona Vale Road (about 3 km back up the road outside the hostel) would take me all the way through Sydney and out the other side at Woolongong, where I could pick up the Pacific Highway to Bateman's Bay, home of my friend, Rod.

The thirty-something girl in my room tried to convince me it would be shorter to take the road outside the hostel all the way into central Sydney, where I could pick up a "distributor" road which would take me over the Harbour Bridge. I'd then be able to pick up "some other road" that would take me south. But, looking at my map, this seemed like a very complicated route and, as Route No 3 didn't involve a single turn, I decided to take it instead, even though it was probably a fair bit longer.

So I set off into the vast metropolis of Australia's premier city. I put myself in the middle lane on Mona Vale Road and pretty much stayed there all the way to the Pacific Highway. This route bypassed the centre of Sydney and took me through the suburbs of Pymble, Ryde and Huntsville, as well as passing the Olympic Stadium.

It was very built up and I took two hours to travel the 100 km to Wollongong. But I made it without incident and didn't have to stop once to consult the map, so I was satisfied with that.

I phoned Rod to advise him of my progress, only to be informed, "Well, it's still another 3 hours from there." God, I should have been used to the distances in Australia by now, but they still took my breath away.

I made it to Bateman's Bay by mid-afternoon, just before the rain came in, so all in all it was a pretty good ride.

THERE'S GOLD IN THEM THAR HILLS

It was great to see Rod and his family again. Back when Lisa and I were sharing the house in Cairns with Rod, Shane and the others, Rod had decided he wanted to be with a girl called Kim he'd met earlier in their travels in Bateman's Bay. He drove all the way there from Cairns to be with her. I cadged a lift with him as far as Sydney, and always thought it was one of the most romantic gestures I'd ever known. A few years later, he asked her to marry him and they went on to have two children.

It was always a delight to see them and catch up on all the changes in their lives. Shane had also moved to Bateman's Bay, so the first evening I was there, Rod arranged for him to come round for dinner. Shane now had a brood of young sons and it was nice to catch up on his news, too.

On the Friday, Rod took me for a drive in his four-wheel drive to Shallow Crossing. This involved taking a dirt track up into the forest for several miles before the road descended to the River Clyde, where a concrete weir had been built across the river. As there had been so much rain it was completely submerged and we had to drive quite slowly across it to avoid being swept away by the current.

We then went up to look at some old gold mines. You wouldn't have been able to tell they were there, unless you already knew. To the untrained eye they just looked like piles of earth, but upon closer inspection you could see that huge, seemingly bottomless pits had been dug. I found it amazing to think that early settlers had carried in all the equipment they needed on foot, and probably spent months at a time burrowing for this precious metal.

Again, my heart strings were pulled, leaving my old friends, but as I'd now booked my tickets home I needed to keep moving.

The next day, I took the road to Canberra. It wound up through a forest before coming out onto an open plain, where I nearly got blown off the road again, the wind was so strong. I'd forgotten about the crosswinds you get when travelling from east to west. You'd think you'd get used to it after a while, but being blown across the road still scared the crap out of me.

I managed to find my way into the centre of Canberra and, just as I made my final turn into London Circuit, a car in the right-hand turn lane decided to go straight on and nearly knocked me off my bike. Admittedly, I was in the left lane, but I was indicating to go right (as were a number of other cars), so I didn't quite know what that other driver was up to.

I later went back to inspect the junction and discovered that the right-hand lane wasn't a dedicated right-turn lane, so that's why the car had gone straight on. It would have helped if I had been in the right lane to begin with. Anyway, I safely made it back to the YHA and then met up with Nick for dinner.

RIDERS' REUNION

After Nick went back to Canberra during our trip to Adelaide, I didn't really expect to hear much more from him. However, he texted me every week or so to see how I was doing, and more frequently while I made my way up to Mount Molloy. It was comforting to know that someone was keeping an eye out for me and I appreciated this contact.

When I left Mount Molloy, I texted Nick to let him know I might be coming back through Canberra. He said it didn't matter when I'd be coming, he'd make sure he was available. When I got closer he even offered to put me up at his house. I was really touched by this, but as I knew his sons lived with him I didn't feel it was the best thing to do so I opted to stay in the YHA.

It was nice to see Nick again, but he seemed a little uncomfortable with me and was quick to let me know that he was meeting up with some friends after dinner. I was quite surprised by this, but as it was a Saturday night I figured it wasn't that unusual, really. I tagged along for one drink, but his attention seemed to be elsewhere so I left him to it.

SPACE MISSION

We met up again the next morning and took the bikes out to the NASA Deep Space Communications Complex. This is where they "listen" to space. I had a fabulous time looking at all the exhibits and taking photos of the satellite dishes, but again Nick seemed a little restless (having been there many times before, he said), so I suggested he could leave if he wanted and I'd go back via the Mount Stromlo Observatory.

Until 2003 Mount Stromlo housed about five telescopes, but they were all destroyed in a massive bushfire and now only the shells of the buildings remain – the actual telescopes were damaged beyond repair. By this time, I was on a bit of a space mission and decided I would boldly go where no man had gone before and find the Planetarium. As I didn't know where this was, I went to the Tourist Information Centre, only to discover that the Planetarium had also been destroyed by fire in 2008.

So my space mission had to be aborted for the day and I had to content myself with going to see *127 Hours* at the pictures instead. If you haven't seen this film, it's about a guy who falls down a ravine and gets his arm trapped between a boulder and the rock face. He eventually has to cut his arm off to get free. And, yes, it's a true story.

MIXED MESSAGES

The next day, Nick lent me a push bike and took me off to see the National War Memorial. It was an impressive building that also housed a museum of wartime artefacts. He left me there to look around and after that I cycled part way round Lake Burley Griffin before heading off to look at the Houses of Parliament. Alas, the bike proved to be perhaps the most uncomfortable one I had ever ridden, so I ended up pushing it most of the way round Canberra.

That evening I met up with a very handsome gentleman called Mark, one of my blog readers, who lived in Canberra. He'd offered to take me for coffee and invited me to stay in his spare bed, but just in case he turned out to be a mad axe murderer, I'd declined the bed but accepted the drink instead. Far from being a psycho, he was very interesting and had recently spent a month riding a Royal Enfield around India.

He'd brought some maps along and gave me lots of advice on where to go next, suggesting a route through the Snowy Mountains instead of along the coast. By the time I left him, I almost wished I had accepted the offer of staying at his.

After that, I went back round to Nick's to return the bicycle and have dinner. He cooked a delicious meal and introduced me to his sons. It was good to be able to relax in a real home again, but I couldn't help noticing Nick always positioned himself so there was a barrier or distance between us. Surely he didn't think I was going to make a move on him?

I was quite confused by Nick. He was the one who'd contacted me in the first place and had been so keen for me to come to Canberra, but then, when I arrived, he seemed to spend most of his time making excuses to be elsewhere. Admittedly, I had called him an "Italian stallion" on my blog, so he probably thought I fancied him. But if he was really worried about that, he could have made his excuses and disappeared out of my life.

He didn't, though – in fact, he seemed to go out of his way to stay in touch. I knew there was no attraction between us so I wasn't expecting any romance from him but I was particularly hurt when he dropped me off at the hostel after dinner and, when I gave him a goodbye kiss on the cheek, he said, "I'd kiss you back but I've got a cold sore coming up."

This has got to be the lamest excuse I've ever heard and was completely unnecessary. I was just saying thanks for all his hospitality and friendship, and his reaction felt like a real slap in the face. But I guess he didn't know I wasn't interested and was just making his position clear.

MOVING ON

Feeling a bit miffed, I left Canberra and took the King's Highway back to Bateman's Bay before heading south along the Princes Highway to Moruya to meet up with Steve, a friend of Lou's. I'd met Steve at Lisa and Lou's when I first arrived in Melbourne and he came over to pick up a bike he'd bought. He was quite interested in my trip and told me to look him up if I passed his way. As Moruya was on my way, I took up his offer.

He took me to lunch at a local pub and we had a good yarn about what had been going on since we last met. Steve was a fun guy and by the time lunch was over I'd completely forgotten my bad mood and was in much better spirits. He sent me to see his wife Jan, who owned a small book store in the town. She, too, was lovely and made me feel very welcome.

It was only when I left her and got to a petrol station that I realised I'd lost my wallet. Panic-stricken, I fled back to the pub, where luckily they'd just found it. God, that was the second time I'd lost it and the second time the good, honest folk of Australia had returned it to me.

Steve recommended going to Tathra, a pretty seaside town, for the night. By the time I got there it was quite late and I just managed to get the last room in the inn – a family room with seven beds in it. Another (very attractive) biker called Mick, who was heading for the Superbike Races at Phillip Island, had just checked in when I arrived, so we had a bit of a chat and tentatively arranged to have dinner together.

As I went off to have a shower and get changed, my imagination was running riot with ideas of what we could do in all those beds. However, by the time I got back to the bar, some other woman had ensnared Mick.

I felt utterly deflated. I slunk off to the restaurant, had my dinner and retreated to my room, with all its empty beds, to consider my lot when it came to love. Time was running out, the trip was nearly over and it seemed like I was never going to meet anyone. Every guy I encountered was either married, separated, fancied someone else, didn't fancy me, had a complicated situation going on or I didn't like him.

And why was it bothering me so much anyway? Hadn't I found the inner love and happiness I'd been looking for, out in the depths of the outback? I couldn't understand why I was feeling so disgruntled. I guess I was finding all this "finding the love within" quite hard work and had been hoping for the easy way out – that someone else would provide it. The fact that they didn't depressed me greatly.

But at least I'd learnt the difference between love and romance. I'd learnt that love comes from within, regardless of whether there's a "special person" in your life or not. I'd discovered that kindness, gratitude and appreciation were the easiest ways for me to feel love, and the more I was able to generate these feelings within myself, the more I was able to connect with others.

However, I discovered I needed romance in my life, too. I needed the intimacy of sharing my life with another and that's why I'd been so frustrated by all my experiences coming down the east coast. It took me months after I got home to figure out why I'd been so annoyed with Nick. Eventually I realised that, although I hadn't fancied him, I had wanted romance, and even though he wasn't the right person, he *represented* something I wanted. As did Mick.

Chapter 15: Getting Dirty

SNOWY MOUNTAIN PARADISE

When I went to pack up the bike the next morning I realised that, in my distracted state the night before, I had broken my own cardinal rule and parked my bike nose in to the wall of the car park on a downward slope. It took me about ten minutes to manoeuvre the thing back out again. Clearly I needed to stop dreaming of romance and focus on riding.

I left Tathra, rejoined the Princes Highway north for a few kilometres and then took the Snowy Mountains Highway west to Cooma and Jindabyne. It was the most gorgeous day – clear blue skies, radiant sunshine and stunning clarity, and I had a joyful day's riding. It was quite cool climbing up over Brown Mountain and once again I had to dig out my windproof jacket. At Jindabyne I turned onto the Alpine Way to Thredbo. This is where the Kosciuszko National Park starts and where the Australian ski resorts are located.

Until this point, the roads had been lovely wide, open ones with sweeping bends and gentle gradients, but after Thredbo the road narrowed and became another tight Alpine pass. At one point a pack of other riders (also heading for the Superbike Races, it turned out) passed me. Round the next bend, we had to stop for roadworks.

One guy looked at my overloaded bike but before he could say anything, I said, "Don't say a word."

So he turned away, but obviously he couldn't resist it, turned back, and said, "Moving house?"

I couldn't help but laugh.

It took me most of the afternoon to get from one side of the Alpine Way to the other, but it was beautiful country and I didn't mind at all. This was the route that Mark in Canberra had suggested and I was extremely grateful for his recommendation.

I took the Murray Valley Highway to a small town called Tallangatta (which is back in Victoria). Tallangatta sits on Lake Hume, which was dammed back in the 1900s. The resultant rise in water level meant the whole town had to be moved 10 km uphill, from Old Tallangatta to its current location. Rather than rebuild the houses, they just uprooted them, put them on the backs of trucks and drove them to their new positions, as they still do in parts of America today.

The local hotel was doing a super-cheap deal for motorcyclists, so I decided to book in. This meant walking into the bar, a dark and dingy space filled with men with large beer bellies and varying numbers of teeth. The owners were very friendly, though, and one of them escorted me and my bike round to their secure parking area at the back – a courtesy not usually extended to male motorcyclists, it would appear. As the Superbike Races were on at the weekend, the place was full of other bikers making their way to Phillip Island.

The next morning, at breakfast, I recognised a group of them that I'd seen at a petrol station the day before. One of them was extremely put out because he'd been done for speeding coming down the Alpine Way and been fined $800 for it. It seemed a somewhat excessive amount to me, but apparently because he'd been doing 120 km/h in a 60 km/h zone, that was the penalty. I was amazed he'd been able to go that fast on such a bendy strip of road.

GETTING TO GRIPS WITH GRAVEL

I had the next day off, wandered around Tallangatta and caught up on my laundry. But the day after that, I wanted to get to Lakes Entrance on the south coast. According to my HEMA Motorcycle Atlas, there were three ways one could get there from Tallangatta: (1) take the Omeo Highway (described as: "The road is generally tarred, but there are some quite rough gravel and rock sections which can be a test for the unprepared" – clearly not a good choice for me); (2) the Redbank Road, which follows the right bank of the Kiewa River (described as: "A simple back road ... so it's a lot of fun" – sounds right up my street); or (3) the Kiewa Valley Highway (described as "... a little on the dull side" – er, perhaps not).

So which one did I end up taking? Yes, you've guessed it – the Omeo Highway, with 30 km of gravel track to tackle.

Somehow, I took the turning before the Redbank Road and ended up on a road that junctioned with the Omeo Highway. As I'd already gone about 45 km before I realised my mistake, I didn't particularly want to go back so I decided it was time to face my fear of gravel and keep going forward.

There are two gravel sections on this road, the first about 10 km, the second about 20 km. The first was by far the worst – there were some really steep turns and badly rutted sections. I discovered that the best way to tackle them was to keep your feet up and just keep moving. On the three occasions that I put my feet down, I found it was very difficult to get going again.

The second section was much longer. It took me one and a half hours to cover the 20 km involved. As long as the road was going straight it was okay, but as soon as it started climbing (or descending) and turning, the two wheels of the bike started going in different directions and I began to skid across the surface. The downhill bends were the scariest, as you couldn't use your power to control things the way you could on the uphill bits.

According to my *Adventure Riding Techniques* manual, the best way to handle gravel is to stand up on your foot pegs and lean forward. This keeps more of your tyres connected to the surface and also means that if the bike wobbles, you don't wobble with it.

At one point a couple of guys on dirt bikes went whizzing past me in the opposite direction, demonstrating that this was clearly the best technique. It occurred to me that perhaps taking things faster than first gear might be easier, but given how hard it was to control the skids at slow speeds I wasn't prepared to take the risk of going faster and having a spill.

A bit further on, I saw in my mirrors another motorcyclist with the full BMW adventure touring kit, so I stopped to let him pass. This was a mistake, as my back end skidded out and I had a very shaky stop.

He pulled up to check I was okay. "Are you all right?" he asked.

"Yes," I said, suddenly feeling the tears welling. *Don't cry*, I commanded myself.

"You just looked a bit shaky there."

Don't be nice, please don't be nice, I begged internally. My nerves were suddenly getting the better of me and bursting into tears was not going to help.

"Where are you heading?" I deflected.

"The Superbike Races at Philip Island," he replied.

Of course, should have known.

"Well, have fun," I dismissed him.

Deep breath, and on we go.

As I got closer to the end of the track, the road flattened and smoothed out a bit and I was able to get the bike into second gear and up to 30 km/h.

As I said before, I've never really considered myself a religious person, but one thing I found throughout this trip was that, if there is a God, then I sure asked for His help a lot.

I made it to the bottom of the dirt track in one piece, only to discover I still had another 50 km to ride to Omeo. And this wasn't easy riding either. The road hairpinned its way down through the mountains, with huge sheer drops right off the side of the road and no protective barriers to contain you.

When I pulled into the petrol station in Omeo, a guy came rushing up to me asking if I'd seen "an old bloke on a BMW", as he'd lost him and thought he might have gone over the edge. In the café where I had lunch, the owner told me how three bikers had come to grief a few years earlier. It was foggy and the first two went straight off the road over a cliff. The third saw the second's tail-light rise up and realised what was happening, so he put his bike down on its side and just managed to escape the same fate.

From Omeo, I joined the Great Alpine Road (the second best bike ride in Australia and the fifth best in the world, according to the café owner). About halfway down and within about five minutes of each other, I had two near misses with oncoming cars, the second of which had me hit the brakes so hard I almost kissed the tarmac.

Realising that my riding was becoming erratic, I pulled over, to discover that I was having another attack of the shakes. I think I was having some sort of adrenalin overload or a delayed reaction to the euphoria of surviving my first sections of real dirt track.

After a little rest, a few gulps of Powerade and several enquiries from passing drivers as to my well-being, I was back in the saddle for a much more sedate descent to Lakes Entrance. There, I found a lovely, very cheap motel, and decided to stay for a couple of nights before doing the final run back to Melbourne.

I couldn't believe my trip was almost over. It had been the best, most terrifying and most uplifting thing I'd ever done. As another biker said to me in Cooma, "You'll miss not riding every day, won't you?"

The answer was, of course, "yes".

GAME OVER

Sunday 27 February 2011 was my last day on the road. The final 395 km from Lakes Entrance back to Melbourne should have been a beautiful ride along the South Gipsland Highway, but unfortunately the weather broke and I got soaked. The final approach to Melbourne meant joining the freeway system and navigating my way through roadworks, heavy traffic and a number of tricky junctions. As with the approach to any major city, this was a nerve-wracking experience, but I managed to find all the right roads at the right times and made it back to Lisa and Lou's house without having to do the 20 km detour I'd done coming back from Tasmania.

So that was it – the ride was over. In the previous seven months I'd ridden from one side of Australia to the other and back again, covered 15,630 km, avoided floods, cyclones and heat exposure, met some of the kindest, most helpful and genuinely nice people I could have hoped for, and had the time of my life.

I would fly out of Melbourne to Hong Kong on 10 March, spend a week with my brother, and then fly from Hong Kong to London on 17 March. Before leaving, I'd have to try and sell the bike and squeeze my expanded load of luggage back into the two bags I'd brought with me to Australia.

Chapter 16: Journey's End

FOND FAREWELLS

After unpacking the bike for the last time, Lou and I took a load of photos of it and put an advert on the web. Then I patted it goodbye and silently thanked it for everything it had done for me, as Lou wheeled it into his garage.

I knew I wouldn't be able to look at it again; it would just be too sad. It had become a dear and trusted friend and I would miss it desperately. We'd done so much together – from the freezing coast of the Great Ocean Road, to the hills and pastures of Tasmania, to the searing heat of the outback and the lonely ride down the east coast. It had never failed me and despite my fear and trepidation, it had been my rock – always there, always dependable. It may not have been the best design for carrying all my gear, but it forced me to become a better rider. And for all this, I thanked it.

I'd read in my *Adventure Riding Techniques* handbook before I left that "there are those that like to go fast and those that like to go far". If I didn't know it before, I now knew for certain – I was definitely one of those that liked to go far. I would just do it with a helluva lot less luggage from now on.

Not that this meant I took much less home than I started with. I tried to be ruthless, leaving my tent and a few other items of camping gear and clothing with Lisa, but once again it seemed that I needed everything and I ended up with the same three heavy bags I'd arrived with. Unfortunately, I didn't have any takers for the bike, so I gave it to Lisa and Lou.

The first time I went to Australia, my godmother had sent me a card, saying, "The thing to remember about travelling is – take half the luggage and twice the money ..." From now on, that was how I'd be travelling.

My last few days in Melbourne were a mixture of freezing, cool and hot weather (autumn was coming). I passed them happily tying up loose ends, exploring the city and reading countless stories to my friends' little girl, Eva.

People kept asking me what had been the best bits of the trip and I would definitely have to say riding to Mount Molloy in nine days in the searing heat and riding over the 30 km of dirt track on the Omeo Highway. These are the bits that gave me the greatest sense of achievement. But really, the whole trip was fantastic and I was blessed with meeting some fabulous people, having a reliable bike and seeing some of the most wonderful sights. I felt deeply grateful to everyone who had a hand in making this trip possible and incredibly lucky to have the good fortune to have been able to undertake it.

Thursday 10 March 2011 was my final day in Australia. I woke up with a sore throat, a runny nose and a light head that gradually got worse as the day went on. I read somewhere that runny noses usually indicate tears that haven't been shed and my God, I had a bucket load of them just waiting to spill out.

At one point, I was sitting in the kitchen, when one of Lisa's dogs, Daisy, came and sat at my feet. "That's funny," said Lisa "she never does that. She must know you're leaving." *Gulp.*

I managed to fight back the tears for most of the day, but saying goodbye to Lisa, Lou and Eva at the airport was more than I could take. For days, Lou had been telling Eva that I would be leaving soon, but it wasn't until I got out of the car at the airport and dragged my bags from their boot that it finally sank in what this meant. As I said goodbye to Lisa, there was a huge wail from the car behind me, as Lou carried a sobbing Eva over to say goodbye. That was it. I couldn't keep it in any longer and burst into tears.

I snivelled my way through check-in and customs, but what I really needed to do was find somewhere I could go and wail my heart out. Unfortunately, there wasn't a wailing wall available so I sat in the airport lounge, bubbling away to myself.

TURBULENCE

On the plane to Hong Kong, during a bit of mild turbulence, I started to feel rather queasy. Never having suffered from any form of travel sickness before, I discounted the possibility that I might be sick, put it down to emotional turmoil and decided to go to sleep instead.

A short time later, the girl in the seat next to me started shaking me awake as, it turned out, I was vomiting in my sleep. On awakening I grabbed the sick bag and proceeded to empty my guts into it. I then managed to wake the man on the other side of me and made my way to the crew station, where I announced, somewhat obviously, "I've just been sick."

The attractive young male steward gave me another bag and suggested I might like to go to the toilet to clean up.

"Clean up?" I queried. It was only then that I realised I'd been sick all over my clothes. I made it to the rest room and, as I wasn't sure which end the next attack was going to flow through, I wheeked down my trousers and sat on the toilet.

A few minutes later, said attractive young male steward knocks on the door. I could barely manage to say, "Just a minute," so he proceeded to unlock the door from the outside and pop his head round. Talk about an undignified sight – there I was with my head in a sick bag, my trousers round my knees and covered in puke.

He handed me a cup of some sort of gastric relief compound and left me a pair of Qantas pyjamas to change into. When I eventually managed to peel off my clothes, I realised there was sick all over my underwear too. I made a pathetic attempt to wash it in the sink but since the taps were tiny and so was the plughole, I soon realised this would be a fruitless exercise so I stuffed my clothes in the bag he'd given me, put on the pyjamas and made my way out.

They took me up to Business Class and put me on oxygen for half an hour, before sending me back to my seat for an uneventful remainder of the flight.

My sickness turned into a rather nasty cold when I got to Hong Kong. I was supposed to be staying with my brother, but the thought of sleeping on his floor (literally), when all I needed to do was cry my heart out, didn't seem like a good idea. Instead, he found me a very posh hotel room nearby for a very cheap price, and whenever I wasn't with him I let the tears flow.

I'd had such a wonderful time in Australia; it was difficult to explain why I needed to cry so much. I'd been the recipient of an extraordinary amount of kindness – both from people I knew and from complete strangers. The strangers knew nothing about me, but they offered me help, food, shelter and companionship. They didn't know that I'd been suffering and I never told them, but their small acts of kindness healed me. And I was so sad to be leaving all these wonderful people and experiences behind. Plus, as my brother kept pointing out, I didn't know what I was going back to (in fact, I was terrified of ending up in the same miserable state I'd been in before I went away), so it was no wonder I was a blubbering, snivelling wreck.

But at least I'd worked out one thing – what was I here for? For years I'd struggled to find the perfect occupation for myself, constantly chopping and changing jobs, but the trip made me realise that adventure is what I love and that no regular job was ever going to do it for me. It made me understand why I was always trying new things and taught me not to chastise myself for this but to congratulate myself for trying to create adventure in my work. My career was never going to follow a standard path and I would continue to keep trying new things until I found a job or occupation that offered enough adventure to keep me satisfied. In the meantime, I could use whatever work I did to provide the finance for my next trip.

HOPE

So I came back to the UK with a renewed sense of hope. All the things that had been weighing me down before I left no longer seemed to be problems. All the experiences I'd had and all the wonderful people I'd met had renewed me. Maybe I hadn't found the romantic love I'd been hoping for, but I'd found what I needed. I'd found myself again and I liked her a lot. I was fun, entertaining and outgoing, but most of all, I was likeable – something I'd stopped believing about myself.

COMING HOME

And then I was back. I touched down at Heathrow Airport at 4.50 in the morning on Friday 18 March 2011. After seven months of life on the road and endless adventures it was going to be strange establishing a "normal" life again, but I hoped things would be different this time. I'd had so many positive experiences – people turning up just when I needed them, the money to do what I wanted and the joy I'd felt on so many occasions. Surely this would change me?

IS THAT IT?

So, would I go back and do the western side of Australia? Well, it occurred to me one day as I was riding along on Lisa's push bike in Melbourne, that perhaps cycling an electric bicycle would be a good way to cross the Nullarbor and go up the centre. So watch this space – I may be back . . .

Epilogue

WEIGHTLESS

Despite wondering if I would ever ride again, the first thing
I did when I got back to Glasgow was to get my Triumph
back on the road. The battery was dead and I had to get
the garage to come and pick it up, but as soon as I got the
call that it was roadworthy again, I went straight over and
collected it. I couldn't believe how much easier it was to
ride than the Suzuki. As I came to a junction, I found I
could lean it much further over before I needed to put my
foot down. It was a heavier bike, but all the weight was
hung low so it didn't tip like the Suzi had done. It was a
joy to ride.

I went for a few runs on it, but life and work were
keeping me busy so I didn't manage to get out on it as much
as I wanted. I thought about doing a trip around Scotland
but things kept getting in the way.

Then I got an email from my Finnish friend Minna-
Ella, saying she was coming back to the UK for the Bulldog
Bash[13] in August and did I want to meet up and ride some
of the way back to Finland with her? My mum was going
to be moving into her new home the weekend after the date
she suggested, and I was going to be moving back into my
own flat the following weekend, so the timings worked
well and I decided to go.

Having learnt my lesson about the perils of riding with
too much luggage, I went the other way for this trip and
almost took too little. I still had the panniers but they were
only half full – this time I only had enough clothes for one

week (even though I'd be going for two). I had a small top box with a few tools, maps and other items in it, and a small roll-bag with the plastic covers for my panniers inside. And that was it. As I swung my leg over the seat and rode off, I wasn't even aware of the weight behind me.

On Saturday 13 August 2011, I headed down the M74 to England, then the M6 to Lancaster where I had a room booked for the night. It was a wonderful ride and I found myself unusually relaxed, soaring down the motorway. My luggage was just a weightless pillion, making no demands on me.

Next stop was Stratford-upon-Avon, where I was supposed to meet Minna-Ella between 12 noon and 1 pm, but I was still thinking of distances in Australian terms and completely misjudged how long it would take. It looked about the same distance as Cobar to Cunnamulla had done on my giant map of Australia but, of course, my UK map was a completely different scale and it turned out to be only about 150 miles. I didn't know this when I set off at 6.30 am though, and by 10.30 am I was there.

Nevertheless, Minna-Ella was up and ready to go, so after saying goodbye to her friends we headed south for the ferry at Portsmouth.

SAT NAV

To make it easier to find her way through Europe, Minna-Ella had invested in a Satellite Navigation system for this trip. I liked using maps, as I prefer to see the bigger picture of where everything is in relation to everything else, but I could definitely appreciate the advantage of Sat Nav in busy city areas. What I hadn't realised is how brilliant they are for avoiding motorways and travelling on less-used back roads. I have no idea where we went, but the ride down to Portsmouth was beautiful, taking us through some idyllic English countryside.

I was really enjoying being back on the road with my old riding buddy again. We had quite a long wait at Portsmouth, as the ferry wasn't scheduled to leave until 11 pm and then got delayed for a further 30 minutes. As time drew on we seemed to descend into a state of tiredness-induced hysteria. All I can remember now is trying to impersonate Michael Flatley in Riverdance.

The next morning we rolled off the ferry in Le Havre, in France. The sun was shining and Minna-Ella programmed the Sat Nav to guide us through country roads to Boulogne-sur-Mer, our overnight stop. As we sped through acres of golden wheat fields and beautiful, rustic villages, I noticed how easily I was handling the bike. I was leaning into the bends without even thinking about it; I was bouncing it up on the kerb when we stopped; I was riding over gravel parking spaces without a second thought. Suddenly it all seemed so easy. What on earth had I been so worried about in Australia?

The next day we rode from Boulogne-sur-Mer in France to Oostende in Belgium. Again, beautiful riding, along roads we'd never have found without the aid of the Sat Nav.

The following day, Minna-Ella set off for Germany, where she'd get the ferry back to Finland, and I stayed on in Oostende for a couple of days before getting the ferry back to Ramsgate in south-east England.

Arriving back in Britain, I no longer had the benefit of Minna's Sat Nav, so I had to take the motorway system up to my mum's new home in Northamptonshire. As soon as the M2 motorway joined the M25, I got stuck in a massive tailback caused by the toll booths at the Dartford Crossing. When I eventually got through that, I joined another huge traffic jam on the M1. It took six hours to ride the 150 miles from Ramsgate to Northampton. If ever there was a reason for getting Sat Nav, this was it. I could have avoided the motorways altogether and taken much quieter, more scenic roads in far less time.

LOOKING GOOD

After a few days with my mum and a few more with my dad in the Lake District, I set off on the final leg home to Glasgow. No sooner had I joined the M6 motorway north than I ran into another massive tailback. A lorry had shed its load, the whole carriageway had been shut and traffic was being diverted though Carlisle.

Minna-Ella had commented that she didn't think I'd be able to filter through traffic with my panniers, as they'd make the bike too wide, but having sat in giant queues on the way to my mum's for this reason, I decided to give it a go. I weaved my way up five miles of stationary traffic to the point where the road had been closed. At one point, I let a couple of guys on Harleys pass me, only to catch up with them later on the slip-road to Carlisle.

The nearest one turned to me and said, "You look pretty good on that bike."

I didn't know if he meant that I personally looked good, if I looked good on that particular bike, or if he meant I had handled the bike well, filtering through the traffic. I didn't really care. All I knew was, *finally* I looked good on a bike.

Further Information

To read the original blog of this trip, view the photo gallery or find out more about my past, current and future adventures, please visit my website at:

www.jillmaden.com

Acknowledgements

My heartfelt thanks go out to everyone who had a part in making this trip the best adventure of my life. To Minna-Ella Aaltonen for giving me the start and end to this story and for bringing so much adventure and fun back into my life. To Lisa and Lou for all their help with finding a bike, putting me up and steering me in the right direction. To Lesley Currie-Sherwood and Chris Maden for all their feedback with the drafts of this book – their enthusiasm and sensitive feedback I shall forever appreciate. To my mum, Gina Gillard, and Celia Richardson for their meticulous proof-reading and to Sheila Glasbey for her fantastic copy-editing. To all the staff at CreateSpace for their editorial feedback and design efforts. To Teresa Flavin for her advice on publishing. To Carol Mayberry for lending me her flat when I got back and giving me a quiet place to write and reflect. To Nick for showing me how to ride the bends. And to all the people who stopped and helped me on my journey and all of those who took an interest in what I was doing – your kindness touched me beyond words.

References

[1]   WWOOFing is a type of voluntary work you can do in Australia and other countries. In exchange for four to six hours' work a day you get all your food and accommodation, so it's quite a cheap way to make your way around the country. Of course, the down side is that you might not get on well with your hosts, in which case things can be a bit awkward.

[2]   Ute is an abbreviation for utility vehicle; what we call a pick-up truck.

[3]   Transportation is the term given to convicts moved or 'transported' to the Colonies. Female convicts were transported to Tasmania from 1803, when the colony was founded, to 1853, when transportation ceased.

[4]   Wicked is a campervan rental company that specialises in campervans that have been done up in a hippy style with psychedelic paintwork, usually including some sort of catchy phrase like "Men think monogamy is something dining tables are made of".

[5]   The last documented sighting was in 1933 (see: http://www.youtube.com/watch?v=6vqCCI1ZF7o for video) but some locals think there may still be some in existence in remote parts of Tasmania.

[6]   Adapted from the Devils@Cradle website: http://www.devilsatcradle.com/content.php?id=devil-facial-tumour

[7]   The La Niña (a periodic climate phenomenon that brings more rain to the western Pacific and less to South America) is associated with record warm sea-surface temperatures around Australia, and these contributed to the heavy rains. Warmer oceans produce damper air and hence more rain. This is driven onshore by the stronger east-to-west trade winds characteristic of La Niña.

[8]   http://en.wikipedia.org/wiki/2010%E2%80%932011_Queensland_floods

[9]   Development Roads seem to be short-cut roads built by mining companies. Unlike highways, which link as many towns as possible, they seem to provide the most direct route from A to B and avoid meandering through villages or towns. This means they can be very isolated and uninhabited.

[10]   Akubra is a brand of hats worn by many Australians.

[11]   The Great Dividing Range, Australia's longest mountain range, stretches from northern Queensland all the way down the east coast of Australia, through New South Wales and into Victoria and covers some 3,500 km.

[12]   Queenslanders are wooden houses built on stilts to avoid flooding. They usually have verandahs and stained glass windows and are painted in pastel greens, yellows or blues. They're designed to combat the extremes of weather experienced in the tropics. Sadly, they are starting to be replaced with brick bungalows.

[13]   The Bulldog Bash is an annual bike show held near Stratford-on-Avon by the Hell's Angels.

Printed in Germany
by Amazon Distribution
GmbH, Leipzig